Shards of a
Broken Mystery

Shards of a Broken Mystery

Restoring Hekate and our Divine Feminine Soul

Shira Marin, Ph.D.

Mute Swan Press

Shards of a Broken Mystery:

Contact: shiramarinphd@gmail.com
ISBN 978-0-9986615-5-1

Fair Use Permissions

In relation to books, articles, websites, and all other forms of copyrighted materials, the author has followed the fair use policy as outlined by Chicago University Press. For these copyright and fair use policies please refer to: http://www.press.uchicago.edu/Misc/Chicago/copy_and_perms.pdf. Readers are welcome to follow the above policies when referencing or quoting from the present volume. This fair use policy applies as well to readers making use of this volume's website features. Please see www.hekatealive.com

Publisher's Cataloging-in-Publication data

Names: Marin, Shira, author.
Title: Shards of a broken mystery: restoring Hekate and our divine feminine soul, a memoir / by Shira Marin.
Description: Includes bibliographical references. | San Rafael, CA: Mute Swan Publishers, 2017.
Identifiers: ISBN 978-0-9986615-5-1
Subjects: LCSH Marin, Shira. | Hekate (Greek deity) | Shadow (Psychoanalysis) | Self-actualization (Psychology) | Goddesses, Greek. | Mythology, Greek. | Jungian psychology. | BISAC BIOGRAPHY & AUTOBIOGRAPHY / Personal/Creative Memoirs | PSYCHOLOGY / Movements / Jungian
Classification:
LCC BF637.S4 .M351 2017 | DDC 158/.1092--dc23

Cover design: Jim Shubin & Shira Marin
Editor: Bob Cooper—cooperite@comcast.net
Book design: Jim Shubin—www.bookalchemist.net

Table of Contents

Acknowledgments

With great thanks to so many openhearted people without whose faith, encouragement, and assistance, this work could not have found its way through the mystery of the creative impulse and into your hands. To Russ Lockhart, curator of dreams, including those that guided this work; and to Suzanne Wagner, who recognized Hekate when I shared my story of the apparition at the bookstore; to Holly Prado Northup and Diane di Prima, who were the first women to read my initial drafts and support my moving onward; to Aftab Omer and Melissa Schwartz who gave me a place to share in academic circles the necessity of Hekate's restoration in modern consciousness; to Linda Anderson Henry and to Aninha Livingstone whose soulful generosity supported my first steps towards publication; to Phil Cousineau, who along with Russ Lockhart were the first men who believed in the work and mentored me through finalizing the manuscript; to those at Book Passage who helped pave my way to publishing; to Bob Cooper, kind, patient, and adept at editing this unusual written form; to Jim Shubin, a truly alchemical book designer, who enlivened the layout of this work with great skill and humor; Laurie King for sharing her book launch secrets; to Annie Danberg, without whose research savvy, organizational skills, and passionate endurance this work would truly not have gone to print; to Lindsay Kittredge, an unflinching companion through this publication process; to the writers and artists who have generously permitted me to use their work, and to my clients, who have trusted me to hold and tend with them their deepest inner experiences.

I deeply appreciate the warm and loving friends who have trusted me in my work, knowing that I would return from the deep woods of this passage with much gratitude for their willingness to honor my process.

Finally, I cannot thank and appreciate enough my husband Phil, my children Eli and Alessa, and my therapy assist dog, Bella Rosa, for their patience and forbearance in allowing me the space and time to accomplish this most yearned for completion.

Dedicated to my husband Phil,
my children Eli and Alessa,
dear Bella Rosa,
and our Great Mother Hekate.

Attraversiamo, Grazie infiniti!

—SM

The modern vision of ourselves and the world has stultified our imaginations. It has fixed our view of personality (psychology), of insanity (psychopathology), of matter and objects (science), of the cosmos (metaphysics), and of the nature of the divine (theology). Moreover, it has fixed the methods in all these fields so that they present a unified front against soul. What is needed is a re-visioning, a fundamental shift of perspective out of that soulless predicament we call modern consciousness.[1]

—James Hillman

Foreword

By Russell A. Lockhart

MYSTERY! MYSTERY! VIVA MYSTERY! THE WORD ITSELF means "seeing with the eyes closed," in the context of initiation. Shira Marin's *Shards of a Broken Mystery: Restoring Hekate and our Divine Feminine Soul*, is itself a mystery, and must be approached as a mystery, seeing with the eyes closed, preparing oneself for ritual initiation. Likewise, dreams—a province of Hekate—are seen with the eyes closed, and this is why dreams too, must be approached as mystery—so unlike how they are approached in the contem-porary world, forgotten, neglected, disregarded. For the modern eye and ear, tethered to computer screens, this may strike one as nonsense, as hardly a challenge to the hegemony of seeking the security of the rational, the protection of explanation, the surety of understanding. But these are not the haunts of the goddess Hekate, who has touched Dr. Marin and placed on her shoulders the task of restoration of this long-forgotten one, variously named "Queen of Night," "The Sender of Nocturnal Visions," "Goddess of the Paths," among others.

After finishing the text of *Shards*—as if finishing were possible—and before writing this foreword, I had a dream as if sent by Hekate herself. In the dream I was alone in a grand ballroom of sumptuous dimension. Overhead, there was a spectacular crystal chandelier brightly lit but dimming as I looked at it in awe. When it went dark, there was nothing to see, nothing to hear, until a loud crystalline crash filled the air and told me the chandelier had fallen and broken into bits and pieces. I knew in the dream, that it was to be my task to repair the broken light.

I take this to mean that *Shards* is "psychoactive," that it may impact you in ways you cannot imagine, do not expect, may not even want, but like it or not, agreed to or not, you too may be recruited to the task of restoration.

Do not read this book as a straight-on narrative. The book itself is like shards, and the restoration occurs with the bits and pieces undergoing a process of assemblage within your own psyche. Read a page. Look at an image. Close your eyes. Wait. Hekate may come to you as "Queen of Ghosts." Or she may appear as "Child-Nurse." Or as "The Terrifying One." There is no predicting. But into the blank space of your imagination—if you permit blank spaces or are able to recruit them—she will come in the old ways, or in new ways, in recognizable form, or in disguise.

I suspect women will have an easier time with

this way of relating to *Shards*. Women are more at home with mystery, more comfortable with letting the "unknown" engender, more at home with the brokenness that is the too-common fate of patriarchy's scourge. But as a man, I must urge my fellow men, do not miss this opportunity to grow, even if the path seems crooked and untoward, even if you can't see very far ahead, even if you can't let go of the rational, the explanatory, the sought-for understanding. Take it on as an experiment. Read a bit. Gaze at the images. Let your mind wander. Under the influence of Hekate, you will come upon the *trivia*, and you will find yourself, even involuntarily, on the branch path, leading away from the straight and narrow, the bright and glorious, leading to the place of dead things, Hekate's realm. Don't turn away. This is the place of deepest psyche, the access to layers beyond layers of deepest knowing. Hekate's realm is the place the poet Rilke, a man, knew: *You must give birth to your images. They are the future waiting to be born. Fear not the strangeness you feel. The future must enter you long before it happens. Just wait for the birth, for the hour of the new clarity.* This is Hekate's doing.

Gods and goddesses, those presences incarnated in the depths of psyche, all demand devotion when they present themselves, recognized or not. What manner of presentation is not our choice. How we respond to the reality of their presence is, though such choices are never easy, whether we choose to serve or not to serve.

Should you be so fortunate as to be chosen to serve—even an unlikely presence like a goddess of old—make no mistake, nothing less than your future is at stake. Taking part in possible futures, rather than having futures thrust upon one, is the best possible course. *Shards of a Broken Mystery* facilitates the awareness of possible futures through the agency of Hekate, and even more so as she is restored to vitality in the individual psyche. This is the gift that Shira Marin, through her devotion to Hekate, has presented to us.

Russell Arthur Lockhart, Ph.D.
Everett, Washington
May 11, 2017

Preface

Hekate: A Word in the Hand

One of the necessary preliminary tasks is to train the "eye for the archetypal."[2]

—Erich Neumann

THIRTY YEARS AGO WHILE RUMMAGING THROUGH A PILE OF remainders at a neighborhood bookstore, an ancient Anatolian (now Western Turkey) goddess named Hekate, in her archetypal witch aspect, surfaced from the bottom of a book stack. (I recognized her as a witch because the book screamed in enormous block letters: *WITCHES*. As I picked up the book, a lightning bolt of numinous energy shot through me the likes of which I have not experienced since. I wasn't expecting Hekate to be waiting for me in the bookstore. Until that moment, the mention of Hekate always and only brought to mind Shakespeare's image of her.

Double, double
Toil and trouble
Fire burn
And cauldron bubble…

Since the age of 15, I have recited these lines whenever a
fierce sense of magic is called for. But the occurrence in
the bookstore was so shockingly magical that I forgot
my lines and darted from the store to reflect on the
meaning of my experience. Hekate and I have a
relationship of some 50 years. She has known me longer,
fostering mother that she is. It may be that over the
2,500 or so years that have passed since Hekatefled or
was pushed into the darkest depths of the unconscious,
she has been looking for a receptive place to dwell.
Vaguely conscious of Hekate's seeking expression, I
realized that it might be my task to help create a space
for her. Thus, the subject of this book *found me*.

From that day on, I knew unquestionably that I
was to follow Hekate wherever she might lead. I sat in
the dusky light of my Silver Lake, California, cottage
feeling a giddy mix of excitement and profound concern
about the work that lay ahead. Blasphemous thoughts
flitted through my mind: "Nobody has ever *really* talked
or written about Hekate in all these years. Maybe she's
not real, not really a goddess. She must not be very
important. She's just a witch and nobody likes or wants
anything to do with witches. What can I say that will
interest anyone?"

Countering these experiences was the riveting
mysterium tremendum surrounding my experience;
the deepest curiosity hooked me. Over the decades

I have discovered, in previously unimaginable depths, that Hekate is so much more a presence than the witch I first envisioned. In fact, as you will see, she is the one who bestows great blessings when she is propitiated with an open heart.

Who's Calling

This path
Leave it …
Go with the tribe
Shake your head like a fool
Stomp your leg like a spear
Rattle your hands til they sound like
Rain snapping against a window pane
Saturate earth until you
Go with the river's flow
Or you can tread the asphalt path

One way leads to conformity
The other, to joy

—Shira Marin, 2015

Introduction

In ancient Greece, gods and goddesses pictorialized
and personified the psychology of those who lived at
that time. Hekate, the Titan Greek goddess you will
come to know well in these pages, predated the later
Olympian Greek pantheon. Though discarded and
long forgotten, Hekate remains with us, a sacred but
unclaimed presence, a broken mystery within the
human psyche.

Hekate is the original triple goddess of Anatolia
and the favorite daughter of Zeus, who was both a
Titan and an Olympian. Zeus's love for Hekate was
so great that he gave her power in three domains:
the night sky at the new moon, the barren sea, and
the underworld, the place of profound traverse. In
these realms, her powers were many, as you will
see; Hekate is, in fact, called *poly-formes*, "the many-
formed."

Of all female deities, the eminent psychologist
Carl Jung called Hekate the true Great Mother
Goddess because when she appeared, Hekate made
things real. In this writing I share my direct
experience of Hekate who makes real the myriad
pieces that puzzle together her profound mystery, not
only as a goddess and archetype but also as a bridge
to a real but often unwittingly demeaned, neglected,
forgotten sense of our humanity.

*I want to show you in this memoir how Hekate
opens a portal and grants passage into the invisible
and into the holy, hidden heart.*

When Hekate appeared to me in an L.A. bookstore, a
tectonic shift occurred within me, the likes of which
only she could bring. Hekate found me and became
absolutely real in the way someone can feel
companioned by something Other. Note that Jung
himself was companioned by his guide Philemon,
especially as he describes this relationship in the *Red
Book*. Hekate and I have been together for decades in
what Jung called the "mythopoetic imagination."[1] I
feel secure in the reality of this sort of presence in the
way one can be accompanied without feeling the
least bit worried about sanity. If anything, Hekate has
brought sanity into my life. She has illuminated the
instinctual life of the Feminine Principle as a saving
grace not yet imagined in the present-day patriarchal
milieu.

Creating a relationship with the world beyond
our ego-driven life is, in fact, essential to evolving our
humanity; it must be informed by the extraordinary
nature of the human psyche, including its spiritual
instinct. Marianne Williamson was prompted to note
that we are afraid of all we might be: that we are
powerful beyond measure.[2] Many people fear the
nature and power of their inner world, their psycho-
spiritual reality; however, it is the natural source of
becoming all they might be.

*I invite you to gently enter into this world as a way
of realizing that the more you engage, the less fear
you will feel.*

James Hillman, the founder of Archetypal Psychology, described it as, "*the spontaneous experiencing, envisioning, and speaking of the configurations of existence as psychic processes.* ³ I hope you will allow imaginary persons, animals, and objects to present themselves and enliven you. This kind of imaginal experience weaves through my story, told here. Without engaging this imaginal world as we might when we work with dreams and other psychological occurrences, it is unlikely that the fullness of our being in the world will reach the depth and breadth of fulfillment that is our birthright as human beings.

A you allow Hekate's being to animate within you, as I did, you may well find direction in unexpectedly resolving deeper human challenges, even those that threaten to destroy us as a society, even when the world at this time can feel, and perhaps is, so endangered. Over the long arc of her tale, Hekate showed me— and now you—how her loss in our consciousness *has been catastrophic*, a major contributor to the state of our lives and our world today.

As individuals and families, as larger communities, and as a global community, we yearn for inclusion, affiliation, intimacy, peace, and freedom. Every loss in these longed for states promotes alienation from self and other. The message here is that we don't have to be united by giving up essential parts of ourselves to fit in, in order to share a mutually nourishing vibrant life experience.

I trust Hekate's message. The restoration of the psychological ground represented by her is a missing link to a future that holds so much more of what we wish for.

The facts presented here are of Hekate herself. They are a declaration of feminine wisdom and authority that belongs to *both* men and women. You will see before long Hekate's firm embrace of all beings regardless of any difference whatsoever. She is the goddess of Inclusion as you will see.

Sharing Hekate's restoration with you is meant to show both her powerful capacity to actually re-constellate in our psyches and to restore and nurture wellbeing so needed globally at this time. For all of Hekate's power, her whirlwinding and quaking eruptions, she sometimes enlivens so poetically that we might barely notice her nuanced presence. Hekate's companionship has revealed her vital psychological energy in many more ways than I could have imagined. Re-collecting her mystery has deeply seated in me what I experience as the final step of the mythological "Hero's Journey," the "Return to the Mother."

I beckon you to join me in your own way and to trust your inner experience.

Many years of dedication have taught me to trust that Hekate is the archetypal key to our shift in consciousness; she both nurtures us and encourages us to develop profound, abiding trust in our human internal processes such as dreams, spontaneous images of all kinds, and the sensitivity of our instinctual life. For this shift to take place, you must engage with your heart open, your eyes seeing. You are needed to reassemble the shards of Hekate's broken mystery. *You* are needed to bring her into life and into view once again. Only then can she support your desire to know the deepest truth and beauty of your whole human being.

It's possible that you have never seen a book quite like this one. I hadn't. I discovered its necessarily different form in the writing as I followed Hekate's lead. In desperation at times, I worked at telling Hekate's story conventionally, in a linear fashion. But Hekate preferred me to see her in pieces, to trace the jagged lines of her fall into the unconscious as the rising patriarchy began to fear the energy of feminine values and expression. Rather than just a page-by-page exposition, this restoration of Hekate's rediscovered fragments appears mosaic-like. It shows a way that the world might actually fit together, to serve all beings. As Hekate makes real your imaginal experience throughout this reading, you may feel yourself living, at times, in a kind of trance, a mist of sorts. These spellbinding moments will immerse you deeply into Hekate's drama. In these moments, you will have united with a most beautiful, forgotten, instinctual reality, one that I trust you will ultimately desire to love and nurture.

One night, long ago, at the inception of this writing, I asked Hekate for a dream to guide me. That night, a dream voice, *her* voice, commanded me, "Stay with the images!" For 30 years or so, that is what I have done.

November, 2017

RE-IMAGINING HEKATE

Hekate Inchoate

AS YOU KNOW, HEKATE, LAST EVENING FELL HARD, and I was afraid to sleep not knowing what mare you would ride across the plain of night. I awoke this morning to find that out of the dank autumn dark you heard my weary call and answered. I beg to see you; I want your guiding hand so I can know you and give honor to your nature. But you have offered curiously only a disembodied voice resounding sure and strong, "Stay with the images!"

To *stay* with the images is to stay with vision, with what the eyes do, but do other parts also do what the eyes do; do other parts have eyes? What kind of seeing do they do? Seeing isn't only the mechanics of the eye. Hekate, already you have hinted at the answers.

But are you visual reality, even pictorial language, rather than abstract reality or language. The images of your face, breasts, arms, and hands are so few. Where are your images; in what ones do you live? What will reveal your nature, your reality? You have left so much to my imagination. Will I find you in unexpected images; will you show yourself in ways I don't yet conceive? Where does this strange sense I have come from: that I will have to see into or through images and words to find you hidden and around them, not visible to the biological eye. Do you live in the shadows or the backlighting of words, in the halo 'round them that hints at the divine nature of the images that live within them?

Image itself contains the old sense of "apparition" most often connected with sacred life and so with you. Your appearance, your apparition in the bookstore, was just the beginning of my life with you. Am I to have more visions of you that tell your nature; will I find pictures, make images with color and words? What will serve you best?

Life is But Her Dream

FOLLOWING HEKATE'S INITIAL VISIT—EXCEPT FOR THE
initial dream I had commanding me to "Stay with
the images!"—I had found no direction.

What images? None had presented themselves
to date. I decided they must be hidden somewhere
and still to come. I needed to stay conscious and
open. It occurred to me that I might need to use my
imagination. My research had begun!

In searching, it became important to consider
Hekate and the psyche in the same breath because
the word "psyche" means soul. Early Greeks, the
Chaldeans, Hekate, actually, and the cosmic soul, are
all the same. So Hekate and psyche are one.

Because Hekate spoke to me in a dream, I took
heart in a passage I recalled from Russell Lockhart's
Psyche Speaks, and decided to record my subjective
experience of Hekate as if it were a modern myth:

> *...in our eager pursuit of past mythological
> images, we may miss relating to the actual
> myth-inducing, myth-producing quality of
> the psyche in our own time. The psyche has
> not abandoned its mythic capacity, its mythic
> generation, its mythic speech. Myth is not
> something that happened long ago and is
> now only repeating, remembered, re-told, or
> re-presented. Myth is not written once and
> for all as if to render all future psyches
> mimetic to stories already told.*[12]

> —Russell Lockhart

Think of Hekate as the embodiment of psyche,
herself, telling her own story; think of Hekate not

just repeating the old but re-casting herself in the story of our time, telling us what has been hidden over the ages and what is in store for us. Perhaps you can group in these pieces a sense of her attributes as secrets, as transmitter, bridge escort, and psychopomp.

Following Russell Lockhart again:

> *Myth is speech of the psyche at any time,*
> *and it may even be more crucial to be*
> *conscious and involved in the mythic voice*
> *of the present and future than of the past. I*
> *believe it may not be as crucial to consciously*
> *"re-vision" or "re-voice" what has been as to*
> *become consciously involved and committed*
> *to experiencing directly the voices and visions*
> *of the spontaneous psyche in our time.*[13]

Thinking back to my initial narrative, Hekate must have arisen from the pile of remainder books to greet me because she wants embodiment *in this age*: the voice of the ancient as it presents itself in the present and for the future. Yes, right now she wants you and me to see and hear her rising up!

Rising up from a mountain of left-over words calls to mind James Hillman's epithet for Hekate as the goddess of the garbage heap.[14] But well-prepared leftovers hark to good nourishment of the past still to be relished in the moment, in this moment that we are now living. It makes sense that Hekate's wisdom and this modern embodiment would arise from a discarded stack of books still to be savored. That she chose this place suggested to me that image as visualization and image created in words, together with the instinctual, somatic responses I have, are her tools.

I will not focus only on past images of Hekate *but on what she tells me now*. How is she manifesting now; what does she want of me now? According to her myth, what must I enact for her? She expects me to witness her constellation of images around me and to express my experience of her. To do less than this is to invite soul-death because experience teaches me that Jung's comment is so:

> *The images of the unconscious place a great responsibility upon [one]. Failure to understand them, or a shirking of ethical responsibility, deprives [one] of [one's] wholeness and imposes a painful fragmentariness on [one's] life.*[15]
>   —C. G. Jung

Jung's message is a mighty weft woven into the fabric of my consciousness. Hekate is now the driving image of my life. Through her, I learn continually to grasp the depths of the unconscious. If Hekate is an embodiment of the psyche itself, through her I learn the nature of the psyche that she is. I am not speaking tautology; I am affirming that psyche and Hekate are one. In that oneness, the images that come are sent from her. I am saying that the modern myth of Hekate includes this knowledge of her. We have a choice to accept the psychic fragmentation, our inner state for ages, or we can take up the ethical obligation of reestablishing the whole of Hekate's image, her essence in our human consciousness. I feel certain, however, that one way or another, *Hekate is bent on reemergence and renewal.* Maybe you, too, would like to come along with me and experience the renewal Hekate brings. I promise you the unexpected.

Big-Soul-Little-Soul: I Speak to Hekate

SOMETIMES THEY CALLED YOU *SOTEIRA*. SAVIOR! THEY knew your power then, that souls are in your feminine hands, that you are the bridge between visible and invisible life. For me, too, a bridge. I call to you: Soteira! I want to cross over and bring friends, anyone who wants to see your presence emerge more fully.

They think you have vanished completely. They do not look for you. You are unseen by earthly eyes. Almost. I see you. I feel you near. Soul-keeper, Soul-tender, you show me where to step. They do not see that you have lain yourself down as a crossroads, as Trivia, as goddess of three ways; you have borne as psyche, their souls, and made for them stepping-stones, created in darkness, a fourth way: their private holy land, *our* private holy land.

You have shown yourself to me. In dreams you ask me to come under the veil of your presence, to look at and listen to you, to make a dwelling place for you. You lead me to look everywhere for you. I see you often when others do not: in painting and poem, animal eye and human heart, in stone, fish, and willow.

I give you honor today thousands of years later. Too long buried in the sands of time. In all this time, who has looked into your eyes and called you: "Mother!" You have reached across the millennia and touched my eyes and heart and hands. "Mother!"

I look into your eyes and find you: deep indigo and purple, charred black, your dogs, Cereberes at the Styx, your houses, night mares, your birds, the swan and the raven, your cat, Bastet, your moon-hare. I look into you. I am drawn through the drape of your chiton into the folds of your holy being. A storming abyss, unearthly riches glinting from within carrying, too, promised death but also another birth. Your cycles: of whirring winding wind—creative impulse; of water waiting in the well-gestation; of heaving life—birth. Mother and daughter, one-in-the-other, eternal-and-earthly-woman. Ritual woman: of Birth day cake, of sacrificial offering for threshold blessing and threshold purging, of menstrual sloughing, and burial benediction.

You are vast. From Anatolia, at Miletus, Lagina, Karia, and Phrygia you were honored. In Greece, on Samothrace, in Thessaly, in so many places, you were honored. They called you *Polymorphos,* Many-formed.

In those days, they knew you one way or another. Now you offer the key to the gate you keep which opens onto your Great Oneness. I will sit with you at the bridge of these crossed roads where you alone are mistress and tend your gate in praise. As the priestesses of the *kleidophoria* glided in procession, key-in-hand, I will hold your key here beside the fire, beside the soft light in the darkness that suggests your nature.

Some Things You Should Know
About Hekate and Me

SOME TRUTHS ABOUT HEKATE HAVEN'T MOVED ME.
NOT yet. Still, they are her arias, and you should
know that they exist.

Not everything I record of Hekate's life is part
of my inner experience of her. Not all of the research
affects me in the same way. Most of what I have
sensed is corroborated later by some kind of classical
writing or archeological finding, but sometimes I cull
these sources and have no subjective reality to
support my research. They may never be particularly
important to me, or at least at the time of the writing
they haven't struck me in a particular way. None-
theless, they belong to Hekate, and whatever belongs
to her supersedes my realm, my experience, or my
search for her or for meaning. Perhaps some of these
findings will touch you in a way that is personally
meaningful. Or maybe there are moments when
great Hekate stands objectively apart from us all.

My Hekate

HEKATE, THE ONE I GOT TO KNOW FROM MY INNER
experience, has been through many transformations.
I have known her from the time when people
grasped the sense that divine nature surrounded
them and filled them: from prehistoric times through
the Bronze Age, close to the beginning of historical
time around 7000 B.C.E.

Hekate existed before the Anatolians and the
Chaldeans knew her as Hekate. Early on Hekate
manifested as Divine Ambivalence and the life/death
duality. At that time the *pithos*, a vial filled with red
color, was buried with the dead. The red elixir was
considered as effective as real blood for the
restoration of life. The pithos was conceived as a
womb in much the same way as the grave pit from
which one could be born again. Not much later,
Hekate came to be seen in her triple sense that
included rebirth and thus the cyclical aspect of
Hekate took its place in the litany of epithets that
describe her.

Hekate is the elixir of my rebirth, the blood of
my life's desire to know her, to make her visible as I
see her, to make her real for you. May her blood
gush through your heart and fill you with
unbounded self-acceptance and love.

It is ever clearer that Hekate has lived into later
history, though in a veiled existence, in spite of
transformations of her outer form and the many
different names, which have been given to her by the
members of cults formed in her honor. There was a
time when she was called by Enodia, and Hekate-
Artemis in particular (this is the Artemis who
predates the Greek pantheon). Surprisingly, village

communities honor Hekate to this day in the guise of the Virgin Mary.

And not only in the guise of the Virgin Mary but of the Black Madonna. The two stand side by side at ancient, sacred sights all over Europe. The qualities of the Black Madonna illustrate a relationship between the Virgin and Hekate: She tends to retreat from directness and meeting; there is a hidden-ness about her (in Nicaragua, she is called Our Lady of the Disappeared). She is able to penetrate and journey without judgment through both personal and collective darkness. She is a missing piece that we yearn for, though we may not be aware that it is she whom we seek. She is a natural authority in the soul's life, the feminine side of our being. She is the threshold of femininity, both virginal and sensuous.

Just think: Mary is the veiled Hekate! In my Catholic education, no one ever told me that Mary's nature was not only of the virgin, birth-giver, and mother but also of a destructress. There was a time when Mary was thought to bring lunacy and was also a giver of vision, a conjurer like Hekate. And at one time, Mary as Hekate was a protectress of vulnerable people, imagined to be a wandering uterus or toad. She was worshipped as a lady of free and untamed nature, whose torch was thought to hold fertilizing power and was passed over freshly sown fields to promote fertility. Mary used to be a Hekate for whom orgiastic dances were performed and the sacrifice of dog flesh was honoring not killing. Hail Mary full of grace, Hekate's grace![16]

In 2009, on Kibbutz Shefaim, in an active *imagination*, Hekate brought Mary to me. Hekate brought Mary, The Jewess, who was one with herself, who stands wholly in her authority.

[Fig. 1]

Hekate Virgine

The only living religious symbol in the world today is the Black Virgin.

—Gilles Quispel, scholar

The black Madonna has been interpreted as a personification of the night-sky out of which the moon is born; she is the ball of dung out of which the solar light emerges, and the unconscious part of our psyches out of which new life comes into being...[16]

Do you sense Hekate in her duality becoming visible?...

...ancient shrines of the dark Virgin Mary draw hosts of pilgrims and often are places of miraculous healing.

Standing near and a little to the left of the light-bearing Virgin Mary of Christianity is the figure of Mary Magdelene, whose name was said to mean "bitter sea" and who, for the psyche, expresses the crucial act of turning, made out of grief and a new vision of life.[17]

—Betty Smith

To the Reader

My task is to make you hear, to make you feel – and, above all, to make you see. That is all, and it is everything.[18]
                        —Joseph Conrad

Before Words

Before words, images were.[19]
                        —Samuels and Samuels

As I read these words, I recognized immediately the truth in them. Looking at the sky, we see the wild horses and elephants, dogs and deer, running through the clouds. Early humans saw them, knew them long before they were named!

Jung Considering

> *Jung (1971) considered the active use of imagery to be among the "highest forms of psychic activity." For here the conscious and unconscious personality of the subject flow together into a common product into which are united.*[20]
>
> —William Yabroff

Get Real!

To say "Get Real!" is to evoke Hekate.

> *To the extent that the world does not assume the form of a psychic image, it is virtually non-existent.*[21]
>
> —C. G. Jung

[Fig. 2]

Grasp Hekate's Presence

IT IS HER SOUL THAT HEKATE CHALLENGES US TO grasp—not all of these words about her, not all of the research over which I have poured, not even *my* experiences of her. All of these create only part of Hekate's image. I will give you a hint: Look with the heart of your eye into the white space between words and lines about her, through and under their surface. Behind them. The task of this writing is for you to see there, too, to open yourself to receive Hekate's beauty just as she presents herself as you read. *It is your human heart-full eye that brings Hekate to life!*

Consider Natalie Goldberg's sense of Zen ordinary, "...the *vibrant* [emphasis mine] ordinary of things as they are." But then let the ordinary puncture your reality; pierce it deeply. When you are shaken by the penetration, the ordinary becomes numinous, becomes divine; its soul rises up to greet you. That is Hekate's presence and her blessing.

[Fig. 3]

Foreshadowing Hekate

I FELT ALONE ONE NIGHT, AND I CAN'T BE SURE WHAt prompted me to pick up vividly colored pens and pristine white art paper. Dazed but intent, I worked and worked until I saw a small island like the lost piece of a puzzle floating in an ocean. Embedded in the jagged piece of earth was a Christian cross with a silver-and-gold cyclone whipping sparks 'round it. On the ground a crown rested against a rock I was aroused by the simplicity of the rendering contrasted with the baroque colors that seemed, really, to have chosen themselves: blue, red, brown, silver, and gold. I sensed a coming: my future inner transformation was revealing itself to me in this reminding image of medieval tarot arcana. Had the Catholic orthodoxy of my childhood been taken over completely, sacrificed by the force of nature? Or maybe it was *to* the force. Gazing into the colors of this emerging image, I felt an unexpected dawning: Within me was the experience of the whirlwind.

I came to know the force of this spiraling breath of life to be an aspect of another image of woman. This was Woman from which religious dictates and my upbringing estranged me. To be woman in this way is to be somehow unchaste and truly reviled by the Catholic Church. To be woman in the force of Hekate's nature is to be related fully to one's own deepest instinctive nature. I was discovering the missing piece of what came to be my deepest sense of myself; this particular femininity was essential to the dynamic wholeness of my being as a woman.

Finding the Goddess

WHAT IS POSTMODERN FEMINIST SPIRITUALITY? IT IS realizing that we don't really need to reach out for statues, mythology, and tales of past divine glory. We just need to listen to our insides when they speak up.

> *The psyche left alone finds the goddess.*
> *No names or distinctions are necessary.* [22]
>
> —Betty Smith, mythology scholar

Betty had an inimitable way of putting forth the most important ideas, and I find myself agreeing with her. But for this journey, let's consider another perspective. Some of the ancients would claim that the psyche is the goddess: Her name is Hekate. That's Hekate deep inside you! Grasp her there, swimming in the dark sea of you, wandering to the surface. Do you see her yet? Soon, very soon.

[Fig. 4]

Unknown Hekate

*Hekate is best known to classicists and
historians of religion as the horrific patroness
of witches. But from the Hellenistic age [356
B.C. well into the 1st century A.D.] onwards,
some Greek and Roman philosophers and
magicians portrayed her quite differently,
allotting to her such duties as ensouling the
cosmos and the individual men within it,
forming the connective boundary between
divine and human worlds, and facilitating
such communication between man and god
as could lead eventually to the individual
soul's release. She was celestial and
potentially beneficent, rather than chthonic
and threatening.*[26]

—Sarah Johnston

Hesiod's piece below characterizes Hekate's
power and nature in three domains. She is the only
goddess in the Greek culture to rule in this way:
born in Mother Asteria's sparkling sky as the new
moon, in chthonic earth, and in the unexpectedly
barren sea. Hesiod (c. 700 B.C.), one of the most
ancient Greek epic poets, wrote what is probably the
most outstanding exultation of Hekate by any
individual at any time. Only much later, at the dawn
of the Renaissance, was Hekate transfigured into the
witch she is envisioned to be today.

*And Phoebe came to Koios' longed-for bed.
Loved by the god, the goddess conceived and*

bore Leto, the dark-robed always mild and kind
to men and deathless gods; gentlest in all
Olympus; from the beginning she was mild
Then Phoebe bore renowned Asterie
Whom Perses led, a bride, to his great house.
Last she bore Hekate, who above all,
Is honoured by the son of Kronos, Zeus.
He gave her glorious gifts: a share of earth
And of the barren sea. In starry heaven
She has her place,
And the immortal gods
Respect her greatly. Even now, when men
Upon the earth, according to the rites, Make
handsome sacrifices, and entreat
The gods for favour, Hekate is called.
Great honours follow readily that man
Whose prayers the goddess graciously receives;
And she can give him wealth; that power is hers.
Of all the children Earth and Ocean bore,
Who once had privilege, she kept her due.
The son of Kronos never did her harm
Nor did he snatch away the rights she had
Under the Titan gods of old; she keeps Her
privilege in earth and sea and heaven as it
was proportional from the start.
Nor did she get a lesser share
Because she had no brothers to defend her rights.
Her share is greater: Zeus is her advocate
Help and success come to her favourites;
In court she sits beside respected lords;
In the assembly of the people, he
Whom she has chosen, shines.
And when men arm

For man destroying war, the goddess helps
The men she wants to help and eagerly
Brings victory and glorious fame to them.
A splendid ally in the games when men, compete,
then, too, she brings success and help. The man
she favors wins by might and strength. And gains
the lovely prize with ease and joy,
And brings his parents glory. She is good
To stand by horsemen, also good for those
Who work the crude grey sea, and those who pray
To Hekate and to the god who shakes
The earth with crashes, get great hauls from her,
The glorious goddess, if she wishes it
But just as easily she takes away
All she has given, if she wants it so.
And she is helpful in the stables, too,
Along with Hermes, to increase the stock. The
herds of cattle and of goats, and flocks of
woolly sheep grow numerous, from few, if
she is willing, or grow small from great. Thus
among the honoured, deathless gods, She is
revered, although her mother bore
no sons. The son of Kronos also made
Her nurse and overseer of all the young
Who from that day were born and came to see
The light of dawn who sees the world; and thus
She is a nurse; and these are her high tasks.[27]

—Hesiod

[Fig. 6]

Upside down

> *The underworld is converse to the day world,*
> *and so its behavior will be obverse, perverse.*
> *What is merely shit from the day perspective,*
> *what Freud called day-residues, becomes soul*
> *food when turned upside down.*[28]
> —James Hillman

I DIDN'T WANT TO BE AMERICANIZED, LIKE VELVEETA cheese. I yearned for the underworld of my Italian ancestors, dreamt of soul food: Hekate's fine cooking. If only I could move to the underworld my acculturating parents had rejected, at least in public.

I remember visiting my "godmother," mom's *comare*, Virginia. It was like going into the underworld; it was where I felt completely alive. She cooked entirely in the Italian idiom. As a kid, I would go with her daughter, my extended *"cugina,"* to her house after school. Always, it was redolent with the aroma of parmigiano-reggiano, garlic, and pasta dough. Mom would come to pick me up but, first, before it was 5:30, she and Aunt Virgie would have wine. Virgie always had biscotti or roasted fava beans. Well, mostly we stayed for dinner: three courses and dessert.

I would go home, to sleep, to dream of living in the olive orchards. Ummm....

WITH
HEKATE'S
EYES
SEEING

Shard 1

Etymology of "Vision":
from Greek: *haides, aides* —Hades, the Underworld
                               —the invisible

from Old High German: *wissago* —seer, prophet,
                                  —wiseacre

[Fig. 7]

The Eyes Have It

IN SHAKESPEARE'S *MACBETH*, HEKATE STARES INTO HER cauldron and tells of the doom that is to befall Lord Macbeth. This is the usual sense we have of Hekate as one who sees: the vision of the witch, dark and foreboding, inspiring terror.

In fact, Hekate's vision is substantially more than and different from this image of her. I particularly like this exuberant entreaty to Hekate from the Oracles:

> *Open the immortal depth of the soul. Let all eyes vigorously open upwards.*[29]

The soul or its "eyes" must be completely receptive to what it is to receive from the divine.[32] We must go to the depths of the soul to find Hekate's vision that is able to see upward, to see ubiquitous, heavenly Hekate.

I believe that Rainer Maria Rilke must have had these eyes, Hekatean eyes. See how Rilke treats us to Hekate as both a dog, a faith-bonded companion, and as the inner visionary of Rilke's own soul: one who can in some ineffable way "share" eyes with the sacred. Does this idea add another dimension of meaning to seeing-eye dogs?

I love Rilke's quote that describes the experience of connecting with divine reality. One can't quote or recall this piece too often. It deserves to be noted once again not only because it expresses so much of Hekate, but because we need to look with these eyes to see the joy that is available to us right now by sharing Hekate's vision.

I love inseeing. Can you imagine with me how glorious it is to insee, for example, a dog as one passes by? To insee (I don't mean inspect, which is only a kind of human gymnastic, by means of which one immediately comes out again on the other side of the dog, regarding it merely, so to speak, as a window upon humanity lying behind it, not that)—but to let oneself precisely into the dog, the place in it where God, as it were, would have sat down for a moment when the dog was finished, in order to watch it under the influence of its first embarrassments and inspirations and to know that it was good that nothing was lacking, that it could not have been made better. . . Laugh though you may, dear confidant, if I am to tell you where my all-greatest feeling, my world-feeling, my earthly bliss was to be found, I must confess to you: it was to be found time and again, here and there, in such timeless moments of this divine seeing.[30]

—Rainer Maria Rilke

Shard 2

Hekate, Antea, Giver of Vision
My Hekate lives in the language of vision
My Hekate lives in the language of the image
My Hekate is the power of the seeing psyche
My Hekate lends her eyes that we might see
her and other forms of life
covered in darkness as in the light of the
new moon.

—Shira Marin

Like a cat I roam and find the nocturne bright, the moon dark; I find you, paradoxical beauty shadow of the sun.

Fingers Have Eyes

In the midst of . . .writing [or any creative
act] there is a seeing going on in the hand
and in the heart, and in the eye. . .the fingers
have eyes in them. E-Y-E. An eye that knows
to put this word and not that word, and to
cross that out suddenly, and to jump to the
next thing. That's all seeing. It's not blind.
[In] a romantic sense. . .there's natural
creativity.[31]

—James Hillman

Imagination is the eye of the soul [32]

—Joseph Joubert

So does that make imagination the eye of Hekate?

[Fig. 9]

Animal Fingers

FINALLY, THE DAY HAS COME, MY DECISION MADE: I AM *not* going to write Hekate's piece in a dissertation format. I am sure that she wants some other form, but I don't yet know what that will be. Just musing over the possibilities is exploding the bonds of psychological constriction, unconsciously bound, mentally squeezed into submission to this point.

I called my friend Jill to announce "my" decision. She said I sounded very settled, somehow inwardly resonant, and that my direction was clear—good signs, she thought. "What led to this moment?" she wanted to know.

I told her about the other day when I was passing from the living room into my study and something drew my eyes to my right hand. I looked and was stunned to find little animals the colors of play dough, crawling out of the tips. I watched in amazement and flushed with delight. A miniature zoo at my fingertips. Where did these tiny creatures plan to go and what did they want? I had never sensed them before, hadn't known they were there. I laughed and thought what a curious, funny expression of what the alchemists called the *omnes colores* experience of the psyche. The image fit, though: A spectrum of stunning hues animated these instinctual beings, which were permeating the atmosphere of my home with great alacrity. They were intent. My friend Louise reminded me of Enid the summer god, called the "image fashioner," who created women and men from the dirt that he scraped from under his red fingernail. My psyche obviously had experienced this creative energy and

was ready to have me awaken to it. Tickled, I went
on with my day.

I recall that later, in San Francisco, driving up
Divisadero Street, I was suddenly overcome by a
voice speaking to me definitely from the right side of
my psyche: "Now you can do the project as art for
art's sake!" What? Art for art's sake? I became
conscious that this was what I had always wanted—
whatever form would be right for her, however
crude it might be. Hekate was a primitiveness that
needed her integrity restored. Could Hekate's
crudeness be elevated to art? It could, but only if she
would bless the work, I suspected. I then realized
that letting go of the dissertation task made room
for the moment of conveying these messages from
the psyche, made room for the new form milling
around inside me. I felt irresistibly drawn into the
generative force of the creative impulse. What next?

Reaching for Hekate: I

IN THE TUG OF WAR BETWEEN INTUITION AND RESEARCH,
I wrestle with a means of getting to know Hekate
that I cannot find in books. What images can I stay
with? I have one image: the witch. I have intuited
already that there is much more to Hekate than this,
and I must find some way to discover her nature
beyond the modicum of information suggesting a

one-dimensional reality. It does not make sense to me that I am called to pursue a psychological dead-end. But perhaps I do have to wrangle with the idea that in Hekate's deadness as forgotten-ness, there is still a glimmer of light, of life; there is no end. I sense rather than a dead-end, the present is truly a dead-beginning and that Hekate is rising up from the dead in consciousness—she is still alive in the present and pointing toward the future. Recall my note about Jung, Lockhart, and Mitchell from the Intro?[36] They trust this sense of the dead calling to us in the present to guide us into the future. This idea bears repeating over and over again so we can feel and ground this instinctual truth, alive in the marrow of us. Sit with me for a moment: Sit with your ancestors, members of your tribe long gone. Sit with your sweet pets resting in deep peace. Feel them with you? Try again and again until you know this place of being. Then, realize that all myth lives within us in the same way. Really. This is the essence of what James Hillman was saying to us in the ideas embodied in his Archetypal Psychology. You can read them in *Re-Visioning Psychology*, a feast for your soul.[37]

With all of this psychological food, I have developed a powerful urge to see Hekate as she sees, to hear as she hears, to do as she does, to feel her hand taking me into an as yet uncharted future. Is it possible to walk with her feet, to feel with her hands, to get to know Hekate from the inside out?

Yes! I have discovered that an enactment called *mimesis* is the name for this project that draws me to it. The word evolves from the Greek, meaning "to imitate." Mimesis is akin to that tradition enacted by the *mystai*, the initiates, at the site of profound mysteries like Eleusis, where women and men participated in rites that gradually brought them into the realm of an ineffable and transforming secret, the *arrheton*. I wanted to know from inside this innermost mystery. I prayed to be initiated by Hekate into the experience of "having seen" and to be, like the *mystai*, transformed in vision and connected with divine life.

This is what I yearned for: to experience Hekate directly, to see "the sphere beyond word and image." Intuitively, I knew that mimesis offers a means of moving towards the sanctuary of Hekate's being. In its essence, mimesis is taking on an archetype in order to experience its life and to participate in it consciously and intentionally. That first day in Crown Books, my conscious life with Hekate began. She beckoned me to her and by whatever means I needed to speak to her nature directly. Albert Einstein wrote: "Logic will take you from A to B. Imagination will take you everywhere." I must begin to imagine. Hekate leads well, I trust; the primary question left to me was how well I could imaginally follow her into the depths.

Reaching for Hekate: II

THE POETRY OF ASSEMBLING THE PIECES OF HEKATE'S life, the "making" of my experience of Hekate into a whole, comes from mimesis. The making of the work and its meaning create themselves out of *mimesis*—that is, making in participation with the archetypal image of Hekate. In the blue stillness of dawn, I am now inviting Hekate daily to fill me and to allow me to see her in whatever outer manifestations she will allow. Only the fact of a very sound foothold in work, marriage, and personal development keep me at all sound during this period. Sometimes, even before I can recite Hekate's magic words, whipped into the whirlwind of Hekate's creative storm, her energy begins to run my life. All manner of synchronicities are occurring: Unsolicited, people from my psychology practice, friends, and acquaintances are telling me their dreams, spontaneous images, and experiences; they are pointing me to research from uncommon realms. My life roils like Hekate's cauldron. It is often hard for me to stay with the intensity of these happenings; only with time is it becoming more possible. Sometimes I am filled with amazement over a brief moment that carries me for days in an almost euphoric state. Other times, filled with the feelings of Hekate sinking into conscious oblivion, I feel low, grief-stricken, even depressed-angry or filled with shame. I try with effort to separate my own feelings from those of archetypal engagement. There are moments when I feel dark, raped of my own identity and reality, when the person I call "I" does not know which end is up or who I actually am.

But Hekate shines brightest in the darkness; to repeat James Hillman's saving grace:

> *The underworld is converse to the day world, and so its behavior will be obverse, perverse. What is merely shit from the day perspective—what Freud called day-residues—becomes soul food when turned upside down.*

And:

> *To be raped into the underworld [as was Persephone] is not the only way of experiencing it. There are many other modes of descent. For instance, Hekate is supposedly standing by the whole time, listening or watching.*[35]
>
> —James Hillman

Hillman also points out that we can have a perspective:

> *. . .that can witness the soul's struggles without the flap of Persephone or the disaster of Demeter. In us is also a dark angel (Hekate was also called Angelos), a consciousness (and she was called Phosphoros) that shines in the dark and that witness [soul struggles] because it is already aware of them a priori. This [perspective] has an a priori connection with the underworld through sniffling dogs and bitchery, dark*

moons, ghosts, garbage, and poisons. Part of
us is not dragged down but always lives
there, as Hekate is partly an underworld
goddess. [36]

From here, "we may observe our own
catastrophes with a dark wisdom that expects little
else."[37] Hillman asserts directly that we need to go
through these struggles, that this experience is an
essential part of what he calls "soul-making," a
perspective that can let be what is, a perspective that
bonds us with Hekate inextricably in the pitch of
struggle but also bathes us in the phosphorus of her
golden torch light. I find myself sometimes begging
Hekate to relieve me of the intensity of her
impersonal archetypal nature, but I implore her also
not to let go of me because there is no way to do my
work of revealing her without her help.

HEKATE
TELLING

[Fig. 10]

Hekate is the Cosmic Soul
(or So Say the Chaldeans)

> *Our bones are lightning*
> *in the night of flesh*
> *O world, all is night,*
> *life is the lightning.*[38]
> —Joseph Wood Krutch

THE CHALDEAN ORACLES EMERGED IN THE WRITINGS
of Julian the Theurgist in the 2nd Century A.D.
According to Julian, the Oracle says that "a certain
divinity sends forth thunderbolts and also a womb
to receive those thunderbolts; the womb belongs to
Hekate, who is born of the father, the Supreme God
of the Chaldean system."[39]

> *From Him leap forth the implacable*
> *   thunderbolts,*
> *And the lightening-receiving womb of the*
> *   splendid light*
> *Of Father-born Hekate, and the girding*
> *   flower of fire, and the strong pneuma*
> *   [situated] beyond the fiery poles*
> *From here springs forth the genesis of varied*
> *   matter; From here the sweeping lightening*
> *   obscures its flower of fire*
> *As it leaps into the hollows of the cosmos;*
> *   for from here all things*
> *Begin to stretch forth towards that place*
> *   beneath the wondrous rays.*[40]

In the Oracles, "lightnings" and "thunderbolts" represent Platonic Ideas or Forms that sometimes were equated with numbers. Intellect was symbolized by fire or fiery phenomena.

Some believe that these fragments describe the womb of Hekate as receiving and becoming "pregnant" with the ideas from what was then called the Paternal Intellect. The fragments portray the sense in which the quality of sacred life is transmitted through Hekate's nurturing womb into the material—human—world. Johnston suggests that the material that Hekate's womb receives is part of the Cosmic Soul.[41] And Lewy notes, "Hekate being the Cosmic Soul, the Womb of her all-illuminating ray may be conceived as receptacles destined to receive the effluence of this soul." So we are left with a sense of soul pouring into soul from the masculine container into the feminine and then into the world. Masculine and Feminine are not the same, but they are meant to be ineluctably tied, woven into each other's fabric of existence.

Concerns about the relative placement of masculine and feminine entities disquiet me here because they give rise to the usual chicken-and-egg arguments over value or dominance of energies. My view here is that each has its equally important task that functions authoritatively and interdependently with the other. That is, one energy cannot function without the complete participation of the other at every level of being as a means of dissolving the hegemony of one over the other. It appears to me quite clearly that the way in which Hekate materialized the ideas *into, or ensouled*, the physical world creates this kind of balance relative to masculine and feminine energies. Try to imagine what different steps women and men might take in the dance of relationship at all levels!

The process by which materialization actually occurs is not known. However, three small fragments give both a sense of Hekate who mediated the transfiguration and some measure of the components of at least one triad:

> *...the triad might hold together all things in the process of measuring them.*
> *In the womb of this triad, all is sown*
> *From the two of these flows the band of the First triad,*
> *Which is not really the First, but that triad where the noetics*
> *are measured.* [42]
>
> —Sarah Johnston

In the Chaldean system, Hekate, within her womb, "nurtured" the basic Ideas and sent them forth, altered, to the Demiurge for his creative use. One of the ways Hekate nurtures and alters the Ideas is to measure and divide them. In this, she is essential to providing the delineation, boundaries, and structures from which the physical world is built.

[Fig. 11]

Hekate-Zoe

Hekate
the first of all
her marvelous womb
unseekable awesome
pours forth a whirling generation upon all
mistress of life
dispenser of it
soul animator of all things
vivifica

Hekate-Zoe
Animator of the dead Hekate
sending forth life-bearing streams
pouring forth whirling generation upon all

Translation: Sarah Johnston

DIVIDE AND MEASURE: THE HEKATEAN LIFE OF NUMBERS

[Fig. 12]

6 Feet Deep Equals 12...and 18, too

HEKATE IS A TRIUNE GODDESS WITH SPECIAL CONNECTIONS to the moon's four phases, so it is natural in esoteric mathematics for those two elements to create a twelve-ness (three heads and four phases). Twelve has a particular quality of being "complete" (12 months, 12 houses of the Zodiac, 12 apostles, 12 points of the compass, 12 gods/goddesses in traditional Greek mythology, 12 hours of the day, of night, etc.).

Hekate is also connected to "trivia" (the crossroads—actually in Greece this was a "side" road entering a main road as in the crossing of two roads), so there is another three to multiply to the moon's phases (dark, rising, full, falling). But why multiplication? Twelve is the most divisible (12/2, 12/3, 12/4, 12/6) of the early number series so it is something "meaningful" in magical thinking. Because the division of the year into twelve months is based on the cycle of the moon, luna's rays are pictured, typically, as being twelve in number (or some multiple thereof, off into the "hundreds," e.g., the Greek word "hekatos" means hundreds or multitude). Remember that Hekate's name refers to the effects of the rays of the moon ("she who works her will").[43]

Hekate, en route to the wholeness of twelve and multiples of 100, speaks her three-ness when multiplied by her underworld number: six. Multiplying 3 by 6 yields 18; this the designated number in the Judaic tradition symbolizing Life itself or *Chai*, in Hebrew. The essence of vitality, of the generativity that we are animated, emanates from the number 18, a multiple of Hekate's sacred force. Experience Hekate as Chai!

Foretelling: Key Dreams—1990

I dream:
I was showing someone how to fit a plug
with two large prongs the size of a Xerox key
into a female socket. A special means or
touch in fitting these together is needed, and
I demonstrate this.

I dream:
I am to open a door; only I have the key.

[Fig. 13]

AH, SWEET HEKATE IS FOREVER GUIDING ME TOWARD
the reunion of the Masculine and Feminine
Principles. Here it is again in a dream suggesting
that, once plugged in, it's possible to multiply what
needs to be read and said, what needs to become
known from learning by those who read, by you, the
readers, the witnesses to this effort on Hekate's
behalf. My work is to demonstrate this by telling,
like a secret, so the words can go straight into your
ear and heart.

And from the second dream: I am to "fill." Just
wait: You will see it as the key, Hekate Kleidophoria
(key holder), Hekate as psyche, has asked that I
open the door. What will be on the other side?
The Future?

I can't help recalling the skeleton key from the
past opening the door to the future. Russ Lockhart
notes that the past can be connected to the future.
Hekate makes clear to me that the past reasonably
ought to be connected to the future. She companions
me with the key, which one after another opens the
door, the portal, the way to deepening our sense of
life.

What key would this be? A skeleton key? A
Death goddess with a key to the future? Lockhart, in
dialogue with Paco Mitchell, notes that the archaic
past can create the future in unexpected ways.[44] In
their book, *Dreams, Bones and the Future*, Mitchell
cites the value of ancient practices—for example, the
ritual of throwing bones—and how these oracular
moments light the way as guidance for what is to
come and, I want to add, to the destiny that draws
us individually and collectively which otherwise
might be missed if we rely only on our ego's capacity
for action.[45]

[Fig. 14]

Hekate Kleidophoria: The Power of Twelve is the Key

> *Twelve...has the ability to bind together and harmonize diverse elements whether they be of the individual body or of the Cosmos. Twelve is the most complete boundary, resembling the causes that roll together the limits of the cosmos.*[46]
>
> —Proclus

PROCLUS NOTES THAT, "PLATO ALLOTTED THE TWELFTH month to the worship of the chthonic deities...," and therefore, in view of the powers of Twelve, Plato supports the concept that, "...the greatest Goddess Hekate closes the boundaries of things within the Cosmos."[47] Proclus goes on to note:

> *Plato's comment that the valiant hero Er was killed in battle and spent twelve days supposedly dead, "while his soul gathered information."*[48]

Proclus discusses Plato's Er: "Er was revived on the twelfth day because it was only by then that he had seen in the Underworld everything he was supposed to have seen. [Er's journey] included the souls who had established a life separate from that of the body, in accordance with the dictates of the number Twelve, the delimiter of all the Cosmos, which are 'folded together into their proper sources.'"[49] To put this idea another way, only then was Hekate finished with Er. Only because of and through Hekate was Er raised from the dead.

Come with me; turn the key another way:
Recall here the *pithos* full of the reviving red elixir,
Hekate's blood bringing new life. The Chai Life! No,
not the tea, but the *Chai:* The Jewish symbol that is
said to mean Life in its largest sense. However, the
deeper truth of Chai is that it means *Alive!* It is the
active experience of living! So, Hekate's message is
not only to raise us from the dead, but to set us in
motion bringing the inner world out, the motion of
breath, of filling up with that substance that
generates something more from the inside out:
Moving from what comes to us via the psyche and
its guiding imagery.

To clarify Proclus, the delimiter of the cosmos is
Hekate, whose domain is the moon, the 12th portion
of the Cosmos. "The powers of Twelve—and by
extension those of Hekate and the Moon—included
the ability` to "close" or establish the limits of the
Cosmos, to harmonize and bind together diverse
elements both of individuals and the Cosmos, as a
whole.[50]

Because Hekate has the power to close the
boundaries of things within the Cosmos, she is called
"Kleidophoria" or "Key-holder,"[51] and is allotted the
twelfth portion (of the Cosmos, the Moon). You see,
it is she, in her 3rd domain: the starry sky at the new
moon. It is she who turns the tide in our lives as if
turning a key in a lock to the inner sanctum of our
being.[52]

The key was one of Hekate's symbols at least
from Hellenistic times. Although scholars argue the
point, Hekate is thought to hold the keys that open

Hades and the "bars of Cerberus." This key is said to belong to "[her] who rules Tartaros" or of the "Lady of Tartaros." And it was Hekate who provided or prohibited access into or out of Hades.[53] Hekate: Gatekeeper. Be sweet to her.

In some Hekatean cults, the daughter of the priestof Hekate carried into procession, as a priestess would, a key which was used to open the sanctuary of Hekate. Apparently the great significance of the key was that it symbolized Hekate herself, expressed her nature.

Hekate holds more than the key to Hades. In Orphic Hymns, Hekate is called "Key-Holding Queen of the Entire Cosmos."[54] I believe that makes her an essential part, not only of our dreams but of our waking lives. It's curious to me that one so fundamentally important to our natures and our day world has remained discounted as primarily negative and cast off into unconsciousness and, ultimately, psychic repression. It appears that in throwing away Hekate, we effectively threw away the key to our symbolic connection and capacity to move fluidly between our conscious and unconscious worlds.[55]

And now, traveler and companion along the evolutionary path, let us go with Hekate, and feel our way as restive souls, roaming.

Hekate in 4 *or* Four into Twelve: Daughter of Necessity, the Key and the Fates

FROM A PLUTARCHAN MYTH ABOUT THE SOUL-JOURNEY of a certain Timarchus through the sub-lunar regions of the heavens, a daemon tells Timarchus that there are four regions within the universe:

> *The first is of life, the second of motion, the third of birth and the last of decay; the first is linked to the second by Unity at the invisible [the surface of the celestial sphere], the second to the third by Mind at the Sun, and the third to the fourth by Nature and the Moon. A Fate, daughter of Necessity, is the key-holder and presides over each link: over the first, Atropos, over the second, Ootho, and over the link at the Moon, Lachesis. The turning point of birth is the Moon.* [56]

In another passage we learn that, as well as being a portion of the universe given over to the daemones, the Moon is the place to which souls rise after death and from which they descend again into birth. A Fate is said to sit at the boundary between two realms and to act as a key-holder, restricting access in and out of the two adjacent realms.[57] In late antiquity, long after the earliest philosophers advanced this idea, Hekate as key-holder was often equated with Fate itself, or the Fates.

Number 10, Number Ten, #10

IN PYTHAGOREAN NUMBER THEORY, NUMBERS WERE generally used to organize and limit space. Ten was considered to be perfect, the number from which all others grew. Ten was particularly effective in limiting or organizing what would otherwise be disorganized space or chaotic matter.

For Proclus, Hekate's power is expressed in numbers—10 and 4. These particular numbers create boundaries and organize chaotic matter by establishing limits. Hekate helps us.

Ten is said to have been born from Four as Ten is the number of dots in the Tetractys, a perfect triangle symbolizing the kernel of wisdom. The Pythagoreans were said to have sworn their greatest oaths by the Tetractys. [58]

Ten and Tetractys were called key-holders because they contained the force that physically limited the Cosmos. Orpheus called Ten the "key-holder."[59] Hekate held keys in two domains, chthonic and celestial—and, in fact, stands for the third domain by serving as the ground that joins together the other two realms. As ten is a "key-holder" and Hekate is a "key-holder," ten is of Hekate. Buried in the roots of Hekate's name, we find dekm, which leads us to the word "ten" and its multiples. Aristotle called the Decad, or Ten, the perfect number because it comprises the whole nature of numbers and determines cosmic structure.

The Decad was called the Receiver because Hekate enclosed all the numbers preceding her. She "is all-perfect, all-effective, and a source and guide sharing in the life of [humankind]. Without her all is limitless, indistinct, and unrevealed."[58] Moreover, the Decad is the subsistence of Cosmic forms and is the sum of the Cosmos and *is* the Cosmos.

Proclus calls Ten the all-receiving, venerable Mother of all because she contains and embraces all that is in the Cosmos. He says that she who places a boundary around all things is said to be unchangeable and untiring because the nature that maintains the Cosmos is, in effect, eternal and indissoluble.

Elsewhere, I point out that for Proclus, Hekate's power is expressed in numbers—10 and 4, specifically—to create boundary and organize chaotic matter by establishing limits.

In the Roots of Hekate: I

HER GENTLE VOICE ORDERED ME:

Sit at the foot of a tree. The tree reaches into three worlds—to the sky; from the sky to the earth; from the earth to its depths, the underworld. Sit there in the lap of its trunk; its roots will hold you. Peek through its fingers hailing the light, but feel down, down, down into the dark. What waits for you there?

Among the roots of Hekate, *dekm* and *gwou*:

DEKM

TEN   NUMBER   TENs   GWOU

HECATOMB

SACRIFICE OF 100 BULLS

SACRIFICE OF FOOD

OF BUFFALO

BULIMIA

SACRIFICE 100 OXEN

SERVED UP TO THE GODS

WHOSE LAND THEY PLOWED

WHOSE LAND THEY TURNED

WROTE UPON LINE BY LINE HOOF IN SOIL

WORD BY WORD

BACK AND

FORTH ACROSS THE EARTH

WRITE   WRITE   WRITE

ANCIENT WRITE   BOUSTROPHEDON

ANCIENT RITE

LEFT TO RIGHT RIGHT TO LEFT

TURNING STREBH WINDING

Whirling   Spiraling   Whirlwind

DRILLING

THROUGH THE OUTER EDGES OF

CELESTIAL AND CHTHONIC

between sky earth cross

deepen

HEKATE HEKATE HEKATE

American Heritage Dictionary[60]

Are you feeling Hekate emerging? Are you seeing her reassembled? Can you see the shards slowly coming together?

I Cast the I Ching: 3 Coins

Hekate, in 3 coins you are a single breath!

IN THREE REALMS YOU ARE A SINGLE BREATH. YOU ARE the power of breath enlivening, informing, delighting the right, the left, and the Hekatean brain! Let us be truly mindful *with* you in heart and image. Let us honor the Hekatean soul-brain within, the creative source with a hemisphere all its own.

Ask Daniel Pink, author of *A Whole New Mind: Why Right-Grainers Will Rule the Future*. His research tells us that right-brained functioning, the beauty of all that it offers, has been nearly lost to us. It is not valued. He tells us that in order to survive and thrive, we must engage the right brain with its capacities in "design, story, symphony, empathy, play, and meaning."

Pink also heralds its return, certainly the *need* for its return. He calls this time the Conceptual Age and that it involves relationship "to nonmaterial, transcendent desires in an abundant age." I appreciate his thought and agree with him in many ways, but I proffer that the heart of the transcendent demands that roofs, food, clean water, health care, and education that inspires as an intrinsic part of a healthy whole globalization must come first in relation to his call to the transcendent. When that work of empathy and the application of all of his other five traits are engaged to create and maintain those just named survival necessities, we will have come through the threshold and into the heart of a truly new age.

I call it the Hekatean Age because it necessitates the reconceiving of the Feminine Principle as vital to both hemispheres. In fact, at a meta level, let's conceive of a third hemisphere as imaginal, as the flow of the unconscious, perhaps initiated by the imaginal corpus callosum: a bridge, a hinge, a river's flow of images—visual, verbal, somatic—that privilege the unconscious and its guidance. This river is the current of, the currency of, a thriving global partnership, individually and collectively, that is the 3-in-the-One, a true Trinity in that nothing is any longer split off: whole but recognizing all parts as worthy. We must learn to thrive on enjoining, rejoining, conjoining differences by genuinely appreciating them and inviting them to become an honored part of the whole. Imagine yourself whole, a river running within you; imagine the wholeness of Hekate, how in her images flowing through you she holds the core of you, all your capacities in every part of yourself, appreciated as One.

[Fig. 15]

Hekate is the Moon in three

The Moon is Hekate, and is the symbol of her varying phases and of her power, which is dependent on those phases. For this reason, her power appears in three forms, the figure in white robes, golden sandals, and lighted torches being the symbol of the new Moon.

The basket, which she bears mounted high, is the symbol of the cultivation of crops, which she causes to grow according to the increasing amount of light she gives. The symbol of the full Moon is the symbol of the goddess wearing brazen sandals. Or, one might judge, from the branch of olives she carries, that she is of a fiery nature. [One might also judge], from the poppy, that she is protective and that a multitude of souls dwell within her, just as if within a city, for the poppy is the symbol of the city.[61]

—Porphyry

[Fig. 16]

Hekate in Three

The Weird Sisters
Poster of the sea and land
Thus go about, about;
Thrice to thine, thrice to mine,
and thrice again to make up
nine, Peace! The charm's wound
up.[62]
—*Macbeth*, Shakespeare

3 and all multiples of three, especially 9 and 12
9 muses
Triune goddess
3 domains—starry sky, barren sea, chthonic earth
(the farthest reaches of each domain)
3-fold time—past, present, and future
3 bodies in one
3 faces in one
3 artifacts—torch, snake, and dagger
3 way, *tri-via*: The Crossroads
3 angles, Tri-angle
3-headed Cerberus

All through our mythology one comes across
three goddesses. What is more, they do not
form accidental groups of three—usually a
group of three sisters—but they actually, are
real trinities, sometimes almost forming a
single Threefold Goddess.[63]
—Kerenyi

Feminine ancients from Greek Mythology:

3 Horae	3 Graiai	3 Graces
3 Gorgons	3 Erinyes	3 Moirae
3 Hesperides		

*The tri-plicity of the goddess is very
important. This is not a mere multiplying by
three, but rather a [simultaneous] three-fold
manifestation; the Goddess reveals herself on
three levels, in the three realms of the world
and of humankind. Thus, the human being is
threefold, having body, soul and spirit, and
the Goddess's three facets are often seen as
corresponding to these realms within the
microcosm of the human being.*[64]

—Adam McLean

Hekate, in the fullness of her 3-fold nature, is the
feminine embodiment of independence from the
masculine being but always related to it. She needs
no completion from the masculine realm and yet she
truly espouses men, and as I say elsewhere, along
with Eros she is the energizing force of the
relationship between men and women—and between
men and men, and women and women Hekate loves
the energizing of relationships between partners, all
partners of all orientations. In fact, Hekate is the
reconciling third, the resolution to the duality
between Masculine and Feminine principles.

Willow Mountain

HELICON IS NOT JUST A 6,000-FOOT MOUNTAIN IN
southwestern Boetia, Greece. It is Helicon from the
Greek *helike,* meaning "willow" or "winding," as in
a helix, which is not only a form but *the* form of
information within the human body, our bodies, that
bastion of the soul of the psyche herself. Hekate.

[Fig. 17]

Wel-3, the word root of willow, speaks not only of the turn of the mountain but of the vulvic opening within it, the place where we can spiral into the cave of the 9 muses who inspire us during those creative storms sent by Hekate. They visit when the intensity of our inner experience is three times itself, hurling us into the Underworld realm of Hekate, who, by herself, can spiral us into our depths. Recall that Hekate is of the spiral: I mean that this particular turning energy of the cycle, of the "psy-clone," the creative storm in which the nine muses participate, belongs to her. And in the churning creative storm it is Hekate, also, who like the willow tree both bends and weeps for us as she touches the innermost life darting out into sky blue and so deep into dark earth. At the end of the cycle, at the end of tears is return: re-birth, new creation, another kind of tears, of joy, of newfound curiosity. Hekate is always leading, always following, always here for us, even within that traditionally masculine monument, the mountain.

How often have you heard the call of Hekate within the mountain of you—in that place where only the patriarchy has reigned for eons? What if we listened, listened for the call of Hekate trying to awaken us through imagination, through the arts of the nine muses and their mother, Mnemosyne, the Titan Greek Goddess of memory, time, language, and words—yes, words—before they became the domain of Logos, attributed to the masculine. Do you wonder how this happened?

Monos: the Furies, the Muses and Divine Paradox

> *monos*
> *they say*
> *made war upon Apollo*
>
> *they say*
> *he was*
> *the first*
> *to think*
> *the furies*
> *were*
> *the muses*[65]
>
> —Diane di Prima

YES. CONSIDER THAT ALL OF THESE WOMEN ORIGINATE from Hekatean under-earth and that in an attempt to bring forth the undefinable or not easily seen without concretizing or totalizing our experience, muses could very well come in a fury. At once they

[Fig. 18]

can inspire but also drive us to and over the edge of a creative limit and create a new one. In the creative act, not we but Hekate draws boundaries, and often they are the unseen limit, the one we did not expect, the veiled part into which we cannot see until Hekate takes us there.

In his book *The Gift*, Lewis Hyde[66] touched the Hekatean sense of the muses in his comment that part of any art is the invocation [of the divine], that we stand with beggar's bowl in hand, in a lowly place but ready to receive whatever is to come next. Yet, sometimes it is very difficult to remain willingly in that inner place. Sometimes it feels like torture.

The Furies, also called Erinyes, are the spirits of torture, avenging wrongs done to kindred spirits but also to those who are no kin but have a claim on our pity—the beggars, the homeless. Those furious Erinyes are oaths and curses, not just in words; they stir up mysterious powers in the body which work automatically once they set out. Stygian souls both inspire and torture creative form into being.

The ensuing creative storm is a fury and fertile a fertile fury, a furious fertility? And isn't there often a curse in the creative act? And isn't Hekate goddess of the creative storm? And aren't the muses, those creatures of Helicon, summit of inspiration, the purveyors of creative juice that wants forever to flow on relentlessly, that do not know our human limit?

Styx and sky, curse and benediction: furies and muses. Not so odd a coupling when I remember both of these as domains of Hekate, when I recall that divine life comes not only through the voice of invocation but out of the voice of silence. Remember, Hekate is the Divine Paradox.

[Fig. 19]

Hekate Daemonae Luna Triangulata

I'VE FOUND MY WAY TO THE KEYBOARD AGAIN AFTER A week of being under the weather. Just before being gripped by the flu, I was working on an abstract, triangular depiction of Hekate propelling Eros's arrow to its target. The form it took is illustrated here. It appeared spontaneously as I was writing the "Lily and Carol" piece that comes later. Wanting to discover where it would guide me, I stopped writing in order to draw. I hoped I would be led deeper into the recesses of my experience with Lily. After beginning, I was stopped but then worked it later with the sense of something coming. I couldn't see that the work was complete until I photographed it, and a blue aura filled in the missing piece.

The image creates 3 triangles intersecting, which creates 9 angles and a combination of 6 points and sides. Spiraling from the exterior to the interior, I counted twelve major shards with a tiny magical 13th, which stands for both the ancient death month of the sun and the flicker of new light to grow on like the extra candle on a birthday cake, which itself began as Hekate's food ritual at the crossroads. All of these numbers arose spontaneously as part of the image and belong to Hekate. The overall picture is star-like and reminds me of Hekate's Titan, star goddess mother, Asteria. But I set these observations aside to tell you something else.

Having recuperated sufficiently to begin working, I again took up my research of Chaldean

Hekate and was stunned by the following (I sensed that my artwork had been detained until I could discover this from Sarah Johnston once again):

> The first associations of Hekate with the moon [became commonplace in late antiquity—no earlier than the first century A.D.]. . . [the two] are linked because of their common role as intermediary or transmissive principles. . . they shared the eschatological function of transmitting or guiding disembodied souls or daemones across the boundary between the earthly and celestial spheres; this is analogous to Hekate's earlier role as the guide of disembodied souls on their way.[67]

And surprisingly:

> Xenocrates," Plutarch said, "set up a system comparing gods, men and daemones to three types of triangles. Xenocrates equated gods with the equilateral triangle, which is equal in all its lines, men with scalene, which is unequal in all its lines, and daemones with the isosceles triangle, which is "partly equal and partly unequal." Plutarch suggests a better analogy: the moon is a "mixed" body mimicking the daemonic race; in fact, the moon's alternate waxing and waning is a cycle in harmony with the varying circumstances of the daemones."[68]

Speaking of the moon and even more intriguing to me in reflecting on Hekate's relationship with her mother Asteria and the daemones of whom she was Queen:

> *Some call her earth-like star, others star-like Earth, and others, still, the lot of Hekate, who is both earthly and heavenly. Now if someone withdrew or removed the air that is between the Earth and the Moon, he would destroy the unity and the communion of the Universe, for there would be an empty and unconnected space in the middle. In just the same way, those who refuse to leave us the race of daemones make the relations of the gods and men remote and alien.* [69]
>
> —Xenocrates

So it is the lot of Hekate to partake of Earth and Heaven and to lie halfway between them as air lay between them. Consider Hekate as white space, and then consider the consequences of excluding Hekate's reality from the human psyche![70]

HEKATE
SHADOWING

Her Dark Cloak

*...We need not fear the 'dark' side of the
goddess. She has her own beauty wrapped
within her dark cloak.* [71]

—Adam MacLean

[Fig. 20]

In Whose Shadow: Hekate-Artemis

Oh, Hekate!
are you the All, the One, the None
You whose bits and pieces are everywhere–
here and there is
this any shape for a goddess?
did the Olympians spring from you–splinter
from you
from you was Artemis born?
or in your mystery have you created illusion
you go behind, dark shadow
before, bright guide
beside, blessed companion

Shall we struggle over who is the older sister
shall we say that Hekate is the unseen side of
Artemis
so that we cannot say, "Artemis" without
saying, "Hekate!" so
that we cannot say Artemis without saying,
"Hekate!"
Sweet Shadow Soul
We call you now: Hekate, Hekate, Hekate!

—Author's exhortation

Hekate: Aphrodite's Golden Shadow

If beauty is inherent and essential to soul,
then beauty appears wherever soul appears.[72]

—James Hillman

THINKING OF HEKATE AS SOUL, AS DID THE PLATONISTS
and neo-Platonists, Hekate transforms from negative
witch to someone essentially beautiful. This is her
connection with Aphrodite. Hekate and Aphrodite
have been seen together in the byways of Greek
mythology.

It is not only Aphrodite who has been called
golden or wears gold. The ancient poet Sappho calls
Hekate "[the] golden shining handmaid of
Aphrodite."[73] In that Hekate is the older of the two
goddesses, perhaps, in their truest later syncretism,
Hekate is the *soul* of Aphrodite! Just as I write this
sentence, I notice a passage that reads:

> *The power of the imagination is without*
> *doubt consubstantial with soul. . .In fact,*
> *with respect to the soul the imagination is*
> *like the soul of the [Hekate] (sic) Heaven of*
> *Venus.*[74]

Amusing typo: Hekate of Venus! An intuitive
nexus with Aphrodite? In finding Hekate's relation
to Aphrodite, her name pours through my fingers.
And as James Hillman notes so succinctly: "Visible
form is a show of soul. The being of a thing is

revealed in its. . .images."[75] Hekate makes herself visible here as the Heaven of Venus. Who in this modern age would consider Hekate in this way? Is there any question that we need to see Hekate or that she wants to become visible, to be seen in her fullness, in the beauty of that fullness, as her whole self? Hillman declares that ". . .beauty is a *[being]* necessity"—and then, of course, so is Hekate a beautiful feminine being necessity.

Shadowing Ariadne: Hekate Prytania

ARIADNE'S ORIGINAL NAME WAS ARIAGNE, MEANING "holy and "pure." Ironically, it is the superlative form of Hagne, or "Queen of the Underworld." Both Hekate and Persephone, often considered to be the same, carry the underworld queen epithet. Ariadne's thread can lead one safely in and out of the underworld because it is also tied to Hekate, who is not only queen but also guide.

> *In the underworld, Hekate is the wardress and conveyor of souls, the Prytania, the 'Invincible Queen' of the Dead.*[76]
>
> — Adam McLean

Hail, Prytania!

Shadowing Hermes:
Hekate Psychopompos

HEKATE, HAND IN HAND WITH HERMES DOWN INTO
the Underworld, was it you who first taught the
Greeks that death could not complete itself in an
instant? Was it you who taught them that their
departed ones transited from the sphere of life to
that of death by a long passage? Did you tell them
of landmarks along the way? They learned that there
is no word of finality for death. They knew that to
die is only to darken and that one darkens and
lightens again and again. Somehow they knew that
death and life are mirrors each to the other. Why else
would they have sent the "killed" sword with the
warrior or tucked little vases into the child's tomb?
You taught them to be proud of their beloved
wherever their path would lead.

You must have taught them the art of death
whose images emblazon ash urns and tombstones,
and fills the air with poem and song; the images
silently acknowledge your way. A poet sings of the
dead one's soul, in memory of it. And for the
unburied hero rolling on the waves, he sings restless
outrage, feels uncertain, and like a swan, asserts
uncommon tones. With the hand and tongue of art
you salve such mighty sorrow; with ironic wit you
challenge death even as your verse hastens the dark
ones into the embrace of Charon. Hekate, lead us
onward across the gate, past Kereberos, through the
darkness, into Elysian fields.[77]

In the Shadow of Eileitheia: Hekate

THAT EILEITHYIA, A GREEK GODDESS, BUT NOT OF THE
Olympians, is thought to preside over childbirth is
well known. But look here, just behind and off to the
left of Eileithyia:

> *Whenever a soul is entering into partnership*
> *with the body—at birth or in childbed—*
> *[Hekate] is at hand* [78]
>
> —Rohde

[Fig. 21]

In the mystery of childbirth, Hekate brings time—
past, present and future—into a manifestation of
human wholeness. She stands by as sacred midwife
to the delivery of the child in whom all that is
inherited from the past and all that will be in the
future converge in the moment of delivery into the
reality of the present.

But Hekate is not only midwife/nurse/fostering
one to the infant. Charles Olson put it well:

> *[Hekate] is called, really, kourotrophos: She is
> the nurse, the nurse of man and the nurse of
> life. Not the mother; the nurse, the rearer, the
> carer, the other thing entirely. And, as such, I
> mean, she is the instructor of all nursing; and
> she comes to the aid of those who need to
> lend somebody care. [She is not the mother]
> —but she is tied, of course, tremendously to
> the Demetrian mother—because when the
> mother loses her daughter it's Hekate who
> truly knows where she is, not the people who
> saw Pluto take her. Hekate knows because
> that's her nosiness, that's her mother world
> business. And she's in and out all the time
> because that's her function and responsibility
> as Zeus's principal daughter. She's a wow, that
> woman.*[79]

[Fig. 22]

In the Shadow of Medusa:
Hekate and the Horse

ROBERT GRAVES CLAIMS IN *THE GREEK MYTHS* (VOLUME 1)
that Perseus (actually Pterseus "The Destroyer")
represented the patriarchal Hellenes who, in the
second millennium B.C., invaded Greece and Asia
Minor and challenged the power of the Triple-
goddess who, from my research, is most surely
Hekate herself.

Jane Harrison notes in *Prolegomena to the
Study of Greek Religion* that Medusa was once
thought to be the goddess herself, hiding behind the
Gorgon mask.[80] Her hideous face was intended to
ward off trespassers from profaning her Mysteries.
As underworldly as she was, let's consider her
connection with Hekate: gorgon and witch, three
Graiai who guarded the Gorgon/Medusa. . . Hmmm.

When the Hellenes eventually trespassed on the
goddess's shrines, they took possession of the sacred
horses. We know of the connection between the
horse and the goddess because an early image of the
goddess with a Gorgon's head and the mare's body
has been found in Boetia.[81] Pegasus, the symbol of
creative horsepower, who flew out of Medusa the
Gorgon's head, illustrates this sense of the horse as
sacred to Hekate. To wit, the horse with its moon-
shaped hooves figures in the rain-making ceremonies
and the installation of sacred kings who in those
times were chosen by and ultimately sacrificed to the
goddess with the declining light of summer.

At the moment I first heard my friend Michelle sharing her life with me and my buddies at one of Lee Glickstein's Speaking Circles, I could feel her profound instinctual energy, generative and daring. Her eyes glistened radiantly, matching her words about children as if she could see into their reality and, then, one evening, horses! Michelle's face glowed with deep, hot fire. She was most at one with herself in the presence of horses.

One faded autumn evening, she invited me to her ranch to be with the horses. Before I knew it, the horses were nibbling my hand hugging my fingers with their velvety lips very softly, welcoming my nearness. The horses and I began a conversation from there; we listened intently to each other and pranced around playfully. Finally, Michelle invited me to lie down in the hay-strewn dirt amidst these 1,300-pound beasts. In a moment of what felt like endless time, the horses gathered 'round me. Can you imagine being at the hub of a wheel and eight horses breathing gently around you, their soft warm eyes relaxing, gazing into yours? Just lie there with me, at the center; let's receive their equine being, the breath of the divine warming you!

In the Shadow of Demeter

Repeating a bit of Prophyry:

> *The Moon is Hekate and is the symbol of her*
> *varying phases and of her power, which is*
> *dependent on those phases. . .the basket,*
> *which she bears mounted high, is the symbol*
> *of the cultivation of crops, which she causes*
> *to grow according to the increasing amount*
> *of light she gives.* [82]

Hekate at half-moon, there, in the shadow of
Demeter. But in other ways, too. She is the hidden
mother who hears the cry of daughter Persephone.
She is the One to reunite the two: daughter and
mother. And, paradoxically, it is Hekate who helps
daughters to find their own ways, ways guided by
her through the Underworld. Hekate is the
protecting mother for daughters whose personal
mothers cannot claim them. Hekate is my mother.

Staying With The Image

IN THESE WEE HOURS, I WRITE IN MY JOURNAL. I CAN'T
sleep, don't want to sleep. I want to see Hekate face
even after decades; I still work to reassemble her, to
reintegrate her by way of all these inner travels and
readings. I can't help but wonder as you read along,
if you are beginning to see her as well? In
conversation with Phil Cousineau recently, he
recalled the Chi-Lites' 1971 rhythm and blues song,
"Have You Seen Her?" I loved it!
     I can't help singing:

> *Oh, doo, doo, doo, doo, doo, doo, doo,
> doo / Doo, doo, doo, doo, doo, doo, doo,
> doo / Have you seen her / Tell me have you
> seen her?*

     So, tell me: Have you seen her? It would be so
beautiful to get the sense of your staying with the
images. How has doing this affected you? Is it
bringing Hekate as a whole or in part to you,
brought Hekate home to you, revealed herself to you
so far? If you have journaled or created art during
the process, let me know. Yes, you can; see the back
of the book.

Missing Piece: Found

Nine days: wandering
terrified, swollen sorrow
Woman struggling to strip purple, green, and red
garments of greed, envy, jealousy
tatters of rage
burn the effigy
render love
from flaming wit
render love
from fiery pity

pray in nines until
the tenth springs
from Nyx
torch awakens night
daughter of Helian light
you bring her ripening
you bring her sugar.

—Shira Marin

DYING TO
BE
WITH
HEKATE

O me, why have they not buried me deep enough...[83]
—A. L. Tennyson

A woman dreams:
I am standing by a grave where a circle dance
is taking place as an invocation to a goddess
I could not name.

[Fig. 23]

Dancing Hekate

THE SOUTHERN FRENCH FOLK WHO DANCE THE snakelike farandole do not know that the dance speaks the presence of Hekate. Its pattern closely resembles a journey to the center of a Greek labyrinth, which, in ancient times, was a vision of the passage of a dead person to the afterlife. Dancers would move toward the middle of a manmade labyrinth to show that people possess the force to direct specific natural events through sympathetic rites. Dancing the farandole was a means of mimicking the spirit of the dead person and helping it on its way. But now all of that has probably gone into the unconscious right along with Hekate. Neither art nor ritual: just a game, an entertainment, an unwitting prostitution of the sacred. But what if we were to re-member? What if...?[84]

[Fig. 24]

Black and Blues: A Song

Don't put no headstone on my grave
All my life I've been a slave
And I don't want the world to know
Here lies the fool who loves you so

—Anonymous

Take two from the underworld of the Hekatean
songbook:

A woman dreams:
I am with two women who do inner work;
we stand at graveside and watch a ritual
being performed for the goddess Hera.

Notice the 3-ness. As the shadow of Hera, Hekate is
the guardian of the unconscious relationship
between man and woman. She is the goddess of the
journey that marriage is: the third, the "Other," the
mystery of conjoining two souls in a life together.
This is so at any point of passage, be it at the end of
this life's journey or the beginning of another: Yes, at
birth, too.

[Fig/ 25]

The Double Release of the Soul: Death and Re-Creation

PLUTARCH'S FIRST IDEA WAS THAT *"…THE SOUL IS separated from the body in the realm of Demeter— that is, on earth; then, the soul is separated from the mind in the realm of Persephone—on the Moon."*[85]

Odd, isn't it, that the realm of Persephone is equated with the moon instead of the Underworld. What might the relation be there? The relation actually comes through Hekate! In the original Greek passage, adjectives used to describe Persephone were actually attributes belonging to Hekate.

Note that the author here, Plutarch, cannot speak of the moon without speaking of Hekate: "There are three special lunar crevices. The biggest one is called the 'Gulf of Hekate.' Here, souls give or receive punishment for crimes they suffered or committed while they were 'daemones' in contrast to crimes experienced while they were embodied. The other two [crevices] are deep and are called 'The Gates.' Through these crevices the souls pass, according to merit, now to the side of the Moon that faces Heaven and is called the Elysian Plain, then to the side facing Earth—'the house of lunar Persephone.'"[86]

> *The daemones do not necessarily remain on the Moon forever; they descend to earth and take charge of oracles, attend to and participate in mystic rites, and both act as the chastisers of men and as their savior in war or on the sea—all the things that gods were*

traditionally said to do, but which. . .new
philosophy taught was inappropriate to
divinity.[87]

Hekate is queen of what is real for her as it
presents itself in the moment, irrespective of anyone
else's sense of what is appropriate. I love Hekate's
sense of authority. She is one with herself. She is a
true model for each of us in our own unique way.

Plutarch's second idea: "The Moon is transmissive by receiving, nurturing, and sending forth
souls. As an intermediary, transmissive body it is the
proper 'element' of souls; in the end, they are
resolved back into the Moon just as bodies are
resolved back into the earth."[88]

Plutarch's third idea: "The resolution of souls
into the Moon occurs when the mind is released
from the soul. When, eventually, the Sun sows new
minds in the Moon, the Moon creates new souls and
sows them in the Earth, which furnishes bodies."[89]

Plutarch's 4th idea: "Earth, Moon, and Sun aid
in the creation of a new human. Earth gives back
what it took and contributes nothing to the new
creation. Sun takes nothing to use in the new
creation, but takes back again the minds he once
gave. The Moon both takes and gives, both joins
together and divides, according to her various
powers. The new body, inanimate, is powerless. The
mind, reigning supreme, is unable to suffer. But the
soul is a mixture, an intermediate thing, just as the
Moon is a compound and blend of the things that
are above and those that are below."[90]

This passage expresses Hekate's bridging function and her willingness to become again and again, to re-create eternally through relationship to and making real the soul's intention. For this reason, creative activity is critical in our lives in all forms, not just in the arts. To express our soul life is to live artfully. However, allowing the arts to come into play brings a playful lightness of being when taken as a vehicle for discovering our deeper sense of self, our soul cave.

Do these ideas speak for themselves without any other explanation? They carry mystical and alchemical weight and are story-like. The ideas constitute one voice from the past being brought forward into the present and point to the future. Maybe this is how we are meant to live: ever generating, one living experience unfolding into another. I trust that we mustn't cut off this vitality for fear of. . . .

[Fig. 26]

Hekate: Goddess of the Liminal and the Borderline—Mistress of the Gate
(Life and Death in the White Space)

IN ANCIENT TIMES, THOSE WISHING TO "ASSURE THE rising of their own souls, advanced the idea that Hekate, by controlling the crossing of the boundary between humanity and divinity, either could aid the ascent or could force the descent of the soul."[91] This passage suggests that Hekate's special abilities and good will were important to those who wished salvation and that she was probably entreated often to be a personal guide by those wanting to cross easily into the next world. Regarding the symbol of the Moon, Porphyry says that a "multitude of souls" dwell within Hekate.[92]

Reflecting on Hekate's fullness, I overflow with a sense of Hekate as a great womb holding souls until it is time to bear them, birth them into the next world. I have sat in Hekate's lap for so many years. Now here I am, with you; onward and into the world. Let's go!

Below, in his hymn to Hekate and Janus, Proclus asks both Hekate and the Roman patron of liminality to "lift up his soul from its wanderings in error below."[93]

[Fig. 27]

Joint Hymn to Hekate and Janus

Greetings, mother of the Gods, worshipped
  under many names, beautiful of form
Greetings, Hekate, before the door, great in
  strength. And also him
Greetings, Janus, forefather, immortal Zeus;
Greetings highest Zeus

Make the course of my life radiant
Laden with goods, and drive away pestilent
  sickness
From my limbs and my psyche, raging round
  the earth
Draw purified to soul stirring rites

Yea, I pray thee give me your hand; show to
  me, needful,
Divinely appointed paths
The precious light I shall observe
When I need to flee the dark race's evil
Yea, I pray thee, give me your hand; lead me,
Worn out by your gales, to a harbor of piety

Greetings, mother of the gods, worshipped
  many names, beautiful of form
Greetings Hekate before the door, great in
  strength, and also him
Greetings, Janus, forefather, immortal Zeus:
Greetings highest Zeus.[94]

—Proclus

LOOKING THROUGH THE LENS OF MYTHOLOGY, Hekate, who presides over the liminal space between outer and psychic reality, holds the key to and is the energy that supports the transition between these two worlds. But implicit in the portrayal of Hekate as a guide across the boundary between life and death is the threat that in some case, at some time, she will refuse to allow passage. Those whom she treats in this way are doomed to remain with her eternally at the point of passage.[95]

What would prompt Hekate to keep souls at the borderline? Not holding to the Western split into between good and evil, I trust Hekate's intention to be something other than executing a sadistic bad deed, the foul work of an evil witch. In any case, we wouldn't find much magic in such behavior. Hekate's holding souls from passing onward must be purposeful. In her capacity as a great womb, I sense Hekate to be an incubation chamber for those still having a last task to complete—those still in conflict. Also, I believe Hekate, in her instinctive depths, carries in her nature the demand for incarnation, a demand for embodying one's inner work, one's core nature—Jung would say one's Self—in order to pass through to the other side. Nathan Schwartz-Salant suggests that the quality of such an impasse at this point is no less than the torment of abandonment. But it can also be seen as a rite of passage for an incarnating Self.[96]

This is the fate, psychologically speaking, of one struggling with the borderline experience. Like Hekate in her many-formedness, people stuck at the borderline appear in many forms.[97] The struggler often grapples not only with the literal life/death conflict but also, and equally important, with the life of the human in relationship with the divine. Schwartz-Salant describes the individual burdened with clinical manifestations of life at the borderline as one who:

> *...is suspended in a liminal transition. . .with the result that a 'gross quantum of affect' is released but without its having a renewing [my emphasis] quality—it does not lead to the creation of 'legitimate goals and values.' The goal of therapy with borderline [individuals] is not to repress these psychotic states. . .but to find an approach that will partake of the renewing potential of the archetypes underlying the general condition.*[98]

Looking again through the lens of mythology, these ideas and most certainly the resolution to the borderline experience involve Hekate. An individual with a borderline sense of life often enacts unconsciously the Hekatean reality of acting as a conduit for others' experience of divine nature. Like Hekate, "this person may have the visionary gift of the psychic or work as a therapist."[99]

Earlier I noted that Hekate became disembodied through the misunderstanding of certain theurgists who evoked her. And it is this aspect of Hekate's reality that becomes problematic for the person suffering the borderline state of consciousness. This person cannot embody, that is, incarnate for herself the experience of the divine, which she does so well in relation to others. Schwartz-Salant states that "somatizations and mind-body splits eliminate the capacity to differentiate feelings and to experience [to internally organize and to contain] conflicting opposites."[100]

Most striking about Hekate's part in the joint hymn above is that different from Janus, Hekate must do more than look into both realms; she must *interact* with them. By reacting to both worlds, the sacred and the human, says Sarah Johnston, "Hekate/Soul bridges the gap between them that she, herself, as Soul, establishes and guards."[101] In other words, *she holds them together with her particular soul-radiating eros, bringing about relationship in both directions simultaneously from the center of her sacred being,* what Jung calls the *numinosum.*[102] This linking function is precisely what individuals in borderline psychological states need to internalize as opposed to serving this purpose for others only. Yet it is crucial to grasp that "no one can *own* this image of union, or *coniunctio,* and its energies. It is neither wholly archetypal nor wholly human. It belongs to a liminal, 'in-between' realm."[103] It belongs to the realm of Hekate. Paradoxically, it is Hekate, who guides and follows Persephone out of the Underworld. In a parallel way, Hekate accompanies individuals in the transit across the psychological borderline experience and back into life in a way that allows not only supporting others but mediating for oneself. We could call this sense of life "enlightened self-interest" insofar as we realize the necessity that deeper, rather than less, self-care creates a greater capacity to help others.

Adding dimension to the notion of the borderline experience, numbers, traditionally, were important borderline phenomena. For Proclus,

Hekate's power is expressed in the numbers 10 and 4. These particular numbers create boundaries and organize chaotic matter by establishing limits.

Following Proclus' tradition, the beginnings of a solution start to materialize for the individual grappling with life at the borderline who can propitiate powerful Hekate, the Great Mother, the gate mistress, for her aid. This aid comes by way of interacting with her who inter-acts even as she is symbolized by the crossing of roads!

Hekate, called "Trivia" by the ancients, has described her authority at the crossroads, which are depicted as three, including the side road, which was intersected by the main road. But with our imaginal vision, I can see that main road extends invisibly, paving the way to the underworld, the realm of the psyche into which Hekate is escort, through which she is protector and out of which she leads. Here, I think of the moment in the first Homeric hymn to Demeter when Persephone and her mother Demeter are reunited and:

> *Then Hekate*
> *came up to them,*
> *in her bright headband,*
> *and she showed*
> *much affection*
> *for the daughter of*
> *sacred Demeter.*
> *And from that day on*
> *That lady precedes*
> *and follows*
> *Persephone.* [104]
>
> —Charles Boer

Hekate, though near, rarely becomes visible unless she is beckoned. She is available to us with affection but off to the side, fore and aft, and in shadow and more likely *as* shadow, dark and bright.

Curiously, though he does not mention Hekate, Schwartz-Salant clarifies that the way through the borderline experience is essentially two-fold—to restore imaginal sight and to allow oneself to see and be seen; one must then bear the burden of that until one's psychic split is healed. The second vital restorative element is to internalize the capacity to hold the opposites for oneself.[105]

Hekate: Smote

HEKATE: SMOTE, EXILED, BUT NOT SLAIN. *BURIED ALIVE.* And we restive souls search for you, cross the plain, out to the crossroads. We are your potential, restless for reincarnation. Buried-alive-walking-dead, ghostly wanderers, yearning to fill up with the life that *you* are *alive in us:* instinctive, sacred, and immortal paradox.

Reader, do you feel her life as I do, bulging in my psyche, like a seed about to burst and to sprout through the earth? I am crossing from the under-earth darkness, blasting through clay soil into life— Hekate, as a new expression, is the hope that springs eternal.

[Fig. 28]

Crossing the Great Water: I

HEKATE'S FERRYMEN OR *IYNGES*, HER MEDIATING
daemones, travel at her behest between the divine
and the human worlds. They transmit messages,
prayers, oracles, and the life back and forth, and
draw the two realms together. They make Hekate's
presence known by leading the invisible into
visibility and the visible into invisibility, by linking
the divine and human worlds.

> *Many of these ride upon the gleaming*
> *cosmoi, having been thrust out; among these*
> *the most exalted are three [the fiery, the aery,*
> *and the hylic (material)].*[106]
> —Sarah Johnston

I, with daemon, snatch material from one world
and carry it to the other; words collide with one
another against the prow of my boat as I limn my
way between two shores: known and unknown, the
realm where Hekate is completely real and the one
where she is to become real.

[Fig. 29]

Theurgy: Hekate's Magic

ALL RITUAL FORMS OF DIVINE OR THEURGICAL WORSHIP considered by the ancients to be magical, when appropriately applied and correctly completed, worked "vertically" to link an individual. . .to god. Vertical theurgy is a contemplative or theoretical exercise. "Horizontal" theurgy involves the use of ritual objects and actions and is appropriate to those still bound by earthly appetites. This form encompasses the specific environment in which theurgy's vertical or unifying power was expressed, whether that environment be spiritual or gross.[107]

Then as now, proper piety and intention, whatever the nature of the ritual, unifies, purifies, and prepares the soul of the theurgist in a way that ordinary magic cannot. In the ancient past, pious theurgists sublimated themselves to the gods, allowing themselves to be worked upon, while *the traditional magician did exactly the opposite*.[108] Theurgy, itself, is not to be translated as "working on the gods" but as "*being worked on by the gods*." [109]

In the present day, this is not as strange a project as it may seem. In fact, depth psychology, in the language of Carl Jung, Russell Lockhart, and others, carries this message in every written expression. Feeling at once both ancient and modern, I feel drawn to holding the inner sense of being worked on and am propelled onward in my exploration.[110]

The ancients noted that *Symbola*—a sacred stone or secret names—were used to establish a sympathetic relationship with a god or daemon.[111]

No wonder I have been drawn forever to these elements and have altars made with objects that feel to me imbued with natural mystery. Is it otherworldly? In the act of creating these sacred spaces, even early on, even without the consciousness of Hekate in my bones, I felt the invoking of divine epiphany, the calling of Hekate, into these altars. Now I have, without knowing, created the Chaldean object used to invoke Sweet Hekate: the *iynx,* the whirling "top of Hekate." Certain fragments from the Chaldean Oracles describe the consecration of Hekate's statue by means of symbola like the iynx. Here is one:

> *When you see a lunar daemon approaching, sacrifice the stone*
> *Mnizouris, invoking [Hekate]. . .*[112]

Clearly, the rising up of a new sense of post-modern feminine spirituality is occurring to restore our body to our soul's life and, in turn, outer life. In doing so, we are reconnecting with Hekate who, as we have seen, is synonymous with soul. As *embodied soul,* we are psychologically re-uniting with her and what she stood for before the renunciation of the body in religion became popular as far back as the second century A.D.

It is no surprise that as a society we are more aware of the need for ritual than we have been in generations, that we are performing it, and that it is enlivening. Looking back, Hekate tells the theugists just what to do to enliven her by making and consecrating her statue: [Find] wild rue, the sorts of lizards that dwell around the houses, myrrh, gum and frankincense, the ordinary *stuff* of the earth, of the body as part of the earth, as matter.[113]

Sadly, as early as the second century A.D., even in propitiation of Hekate, in her primordial femininity, some theurgical salvationists required control over or denial of the body's needs. How important the dichotomy became culturally is visible in the following:

> *Do not incline to the somber world*
> *under which is spread the formless, shapeless*
> * depth,*
> *wrapped in the darkness of filth, delighting in*
> * images, without intellect*
> *precipitous, eternally twisting around its own*
> * maimed depths,*
> *always marrying a form invisible, inert,*
> *without pneuma.*[114]

And again:

> *Many are swept away by the crooked streams*
> *of matter.*[115]

How can Hekate be fully engaged in the present without valuing the life of the body and matter? Isn't this tantamount to inviting Hekate's divinity to rise again, devoid of her essential instinctual femininity? It is as if the ancients beckoned only a part of her as time flowed on and eventually became unconscious of Hekate as body. Hekate *is* body.

Hekate's resurrection at this time relates to this

very point: that she wants to exhume her body from our unconscious psychological grave by reminding us of her *full* nature. Remember the seed bulging from my psyche? No worries if you do not. The point remains that something instinctual in us yearns to connect with this fullness of ourselves, and through ritual, we can respond to this yearning.

Because ritual renews value in our lived experience, it is taking on renewed value and meaning in the world. Ritual is not only the province of institutions such as religion. It is the province of the heart, of sentiment, from a place of deeper perception of what is of utmost importance to us.

From experience, I know that rituals of starched wafers and even the more elemental wine don't quite evoke the same experience as house lizards and wild rue as impulses to our true depth—or maybe they do! Whatever the image, in those who grasp a deep sense of the ritual involved, there is a much more profound connection to the spiritual journey that one desires and that, in fact, matches our mostly unconscious wish to own our oneness with whatever you call the divine nature of life.

To return to the realm of house lizards and wild rue, if we are to invite Hekate, we must reckon with basic instinct and the profanity of matter that we are. Dare I say the animal that we are? Humans are animals who we need to cherish rather than make extinct with our lesser-being antics. We must consciously grasp our instinctual life, our animal self, to inaugurate a truly new, truly whole experience of our human being. In this embrace, we link also to our essential divine reality, that sense of Hekate alive in us.

Crossing the bridge to this other landscape of Self, requires us to transgress the taboo of odor, the curse of the animal world that aspect of our nature we have sought to stamp out at all costs. Hekate urges us to let go the *overly* sanitized world that we have created to the detriment of our human well-being, that of other animals, and the planet. We, in fact, have declared unwitting warfare by massively decimating our animal world every day beyond our comprehension, by making whole extinct species extinct![116] As it turns out, the civilized side of us has become a more predatory beast than our animal selves!

After Magic Words—
Hekate to the Magician:

'Make My Way'

Make me a statue, purified as I shall teach you.
Make the form from savage rue, and then add
little creatures—
    domestic lizards—as adornments.
And kneading with these animals a mixture of
myrrh and gum and incense,
and going outside under the crescent moon,
Finish this imprecation, praying it yourself
Take as many lizards as are my forms
    and do all things as I command you with care.
Make a spacious house for me with laurel
branches.

[Fig. 30]

*Then offer many prayers to my image, and in
your sleep you
        will see me near.*[117]

Hekate appears to a theurgist to teach him
theurgical practices beyond his knowledge. It seems
that animating Hekate's statue is a favorite pursuit
of theurgists and magicians and has been so since
late antiquity.

Official list of *symbola* used in operations to
invoke Hekate:

animals
leaves stones plants roots
gemstones
scents
engraved incantations[118]

Ah! Many-formed: Now I can see what brings
these elements that fill my house. For years, in every
room, granite, willow, birds, raccoons, dogs, snakes,
heaved life: altar objects that I couldn't leave on the
beach, in the park, or on a shelf in some out-of-the-
way shop. Before now, I haven't known where the
feelings for these objects came from. What makes
these objects so precious to me is undeniable:
Hekate.

Dear beloved Hekate, my life is your altar.

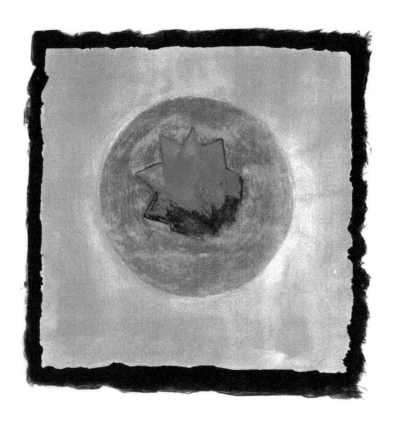

[Fig. 31]

The Iynx: Hekate's Top

I HAVE DANCED FOR YOU IN SECRET. YOU ARISE BETWEEN the lines of reading that draw me to you. I feel you tug at my inertia. Beckoned out of its seated mass, my body gets your rhythm; my arms snake out into space reaching for you this way to the floor and that way to the wall, the corner, and ceiling. Hooting steps and turns take; I make the hoary unheard sounds. Your magic rite through mouth and feet. I twist in your whirling womb, your gold and sapphire iynx. Dancing Wom(b)-an beast, dancing wo-Man beast, dancing woman-beast with thong and sphere whirring over heart and head, reaching out to catch your eye, reaching out-to, reaching into holy life.

Years after making an image, which I thought was related to Hekate but held no particular meaning, I have discovered the following:

> Hekate's top is a golden ball, formed around a sapphire, whirled around by means of a rawhide thong, with characters [engraved] all over it. Whirling it, the theurgists used to make invocations. And they were accustomed to calling these [tops] "iynges" whether they were spherical, triangular or some other shape. Whirling them, [the whirlers] gave forth indiscriminatesounds, or sounds like a beast, laughing and whipping theair. [The Oracle] teaches that the movement of the

> *top, having an ineffable power, works the rite. It is called "Hekate's Top": because it is consecrated to Hekate.*[119]

Damascious supports Psellus and offers further description: "being whirled *inwardly*, this tool [the iynx] calls forth the gods; *outwardly*, it sends them away (italics mine)." [120]

Hekate is considered the transmitter of "spinning generation," which refers to her capacity "to control dispersal of the divided Ideas/iynges that descend, whirring and whistling, over the entire physical Cosmos." In Hekatean magic (theurgy), the iynx—wheel—whose whirling and sounds both symbolize and strengthen cosmic sympathy, are worked only by Hekate's grace.[121]

Recall here that "iynges" are also the names of the daemon-like entities in the Chaldean system. Damascious tells us they function as "ferrymen" in that they [transit] and transmit all things from the non-material sphere to the material one and back again.[122]

More interesting to me is that their transmitting function is the derivation of the word "iynx," which comes from the verbs "shout," "yell," or "cry out." Other derivatives include "a shout of joy or pain" and" a singer or piper." In keeping with the word's roots, the tool itself made high-pitched whistling sounds; its tone was at least as important as its motion.

Following the ancients, wouldn't Hekate want to see us turning, like the Sufi dervishes, humming as they do? You can see this exact iynx dance in

"Meetings with Remarkable Men," a 1979 film about the life of G. I. Gurdjieff, who learned from the monks of the Sarmoung Brotherhood.[123] I twirl, fixing my eye on the horizon. You can, as well. Try: Feel, hear, know Hekate inside you, with you, in your heart. Try often; see what happens!

Myths tell the origin of an iynx-bird; these birds reflect the importance of the iynx's ability to make sounds, to cry out, and to give voice to Hekate. In some accounts, Echo is the mother of a nymph, Iynx, who enchants Zeus. As you might guess, Hera turns her into an unattractive creature, an iynx-bird, which seducers often use as a magic tool. Another account of the iynx-bird notes that, after a singing contest with the Muses, each of the Emathides was turned into a different bird, one of which was the iynx. So, iynx "is born from sound—either from Persuasion, the personification of compellingly attractive sound, or Echo, whose sound has the reflective, almost magical effect of giving back to the speaker what he gave forth. As well, ". . .the iynx is equated with a nymph whose singing rivals that of the Muses."[124]

Turning to the field of magic, the Magi of Greco-Roman antiquity, magnificent magicians, were called iynges, "tongues of the gods," because the iynges transmitted divine knowledge or oracles to humanity. It was the job of the Magi to maintain the iynges, to harmonize or attune them so that they could be brought into the correct relationship with immortal and mortal beings. The Magi thought that the power of sound had a quality of persuasion that established a magical bond of love between two individuals. Others took the relationship to occur between deities and humans such that the human worshipper would be attracted or changed through joy. Magi attempted to persuade and attract Hekate with unutterable prayer to bind herself to them for a time.

Hekate Herself Speaks:

After the dawn, limitless, filled with the stars,
I leave the undefiled, immense home of God
and come to the nourishing earth, at your
orders and by the persuasion of your
ineffable prayers,with which a mortal enjoys
charming the spirits of the immortals.

—Hekate

Hekate comes to me, her voice, a breeze; her incantation plucks a resonant chord within me. I am filled with the sense that Hekate is willing, truly, to be touched by my openness to her. She will commune with me even if not always, as you are about to see!

[Fig. 32]

A Goddess at Your Beck-and-Call?
. . .Really!

Why do you call me, the goddess Hekate,
here from the swift aether by means of god-
compelling necessity.
Easily dragging some of these unwilling
[divinities]
from the aether
by means of ineffable iynges,
you lead them earthwards;
but others, who are mounted on the middle
winds,
apart from the divine fire, you send to
mortals
just like ominous dreams, treating these
daemones outrageously.
Listen to me, although I do not wish [to
speak],
as you have bound me to necessity.[125]

Hear how Hekate is invoked most often through prayer as opposed to coercion? But failing to get what they pray for, the ancients, like the rest of us, are not above begging! As you might expect, with all of Hekate's popularity, she has many calling her name. But we shouldn't be surprised: *My* Magicians and theurgists are *supposed* to work with the consent and the cooperation of my dog, Ginger, who doesn't always come when I call her, either!

[Fig. 33]

Words After Magic Words

Having spoken these things, you will behold a fire
leaping skittishly like a child over the aery waves;
or a fire without form, from which a voice emerges;
or a rich light, whirring around the field in a spiral.
But [it is also possible] that you will see a horse
flashing
more brightly than light,
or a child mounted on the swift back of a horse
a fiery child or a child covered with gold, or yet a
naked child;
or even a child shooting arrows, standing upon the
horse's back.[126]

If you say this to me many times, you will observe
all things
growing dark,
For the curved bulk of the Heavens disappears
and the stars do not shine; the light of the Moon is
hidden
and the earth does not stand steady. All things are
revealed in lightning[127]

But when you see the sacred fire without form,
shining skittishly throughout the depths of the
Cosmos,
Listen to the voice of the fire.[128]

In her formless speaking fire, is Hekate not awe-inspiringly beautiful?

If you should be so fortunate, you might be graced with her favor.

I dream:

An earthquake shook and split the earth. I view it as if looking through a semi fish-eye lens. The earth split into rivulets, and I have to jump stride over the corridor with relative ease.

Hekate's Ephiphany: Hers, Mine, all of Ours!

In her formless speaking fire, is not Hekate awe-inspiringly beautiful? Feeling infused with Hekate's energy, being her instrument so to speak, I have felt quite clearly Hekate's coming; for me, she arrived long ago. For others, I cannot say. Most of the time Hekate is so subtle that in our culture it becomes impossible for almost anyone to find her if they do not know for whom they are looking.

Then, lo and behold, we had the Loma Prieta earthquake (San Francisco, October 17, 1989); perhaps only incidentally it was my birthday. I was very ill for three days prior and was having a body treatment, a gift to myself for my birthday, when it

struck. While Jill, my friend and true Jin Shin Jyutsu
master was giving me a treatment, her dog, Tigger,
who hardly ever appeared after greeting me at the
front door, wouldn't leave us. In true Hekatean
form, he sat in the doorway to the treatment room,
having already been shooed away three times. I got
off the table and as I was passing through the
doorway where he had been standing (5:04 p.m.),
the house began to rumble fiercely; the street rolled;
vases flew and crashed. Jill and I clung to the
doorposts with all of our strength. Moments later,
we felt safe again. Sort of.

Had the ever-alert Tigger known all of this time
prior? At quake time, I hadn't yet learned to speak
"dog." My own dog, a Chow Chow named Ginger,
was only a moon in her mother's belly at that time!
She was born not even a month later. I have no
doubt that Tigger was clueing us in to Hekate's
coming, on her way to erupting into our lives when
something fundamental needs to change.

We and our home, built on a granite hill, were
slightly shaken. Our only breakage was the goddess
of Knossis, who snapped cleanly in half at her wasp
of a waist. I was so profoundly struck by the
experience that dreams seemed hardly necessary.
A month later I dreamt that the earth had broken
open, leaving a gigantic fissure, but somehow I
navigated it with ease.

To some, however, Hekate brought great woe.
At my office, I worked with others through the
anguish of their loss and grief. A client's home was
completely devastated. Between this eruption and
grieving, there was a small noticing of how much

this person's life had needed to change. We had spoken of it together for some time. Ultimately, it was taken out of that person's hands. I know from my own life with Hekate what she will resort to in order to communicate with us, how she thinks we need to be shaken up. I am concerned about the fate of San Francisco, where I am writing this book, and deeply concerned about our country and our world, where war has become a habit.

It seems we haven't listened at all well to a message for dramatic change in the way we run our government to be our support rather than our slave master. Will someone, a woman perhaps, come along with a different sensibility, a view of care over financial gain? Can someone come along to create a sense of village where we all take care, where we engage our service agencies that would take care of Hekate's special children, the poor and homeless, anyone "othered" in discriminatory ways? What will happen next to the soulful city of St. Francis and, by extension, the city of animals, of instinct, and so of Hekate? What will happen to the instinctual life of our country, our planet? Hekate's return, her particular feminine way, could shake us awake to the deep importance, the generativity, of the life force we are! She has done that very thing in my life. Let her do that for you. Feel and see what happens, and let me know!

> *In her formless, speaking fire is Hekate not*
> *awe-inspiringly beautiful?*
> *In her formless, speaking fire is Hekate not*
> *awe-inspiringly beautiful?*
> *In her formless, speaking fire is Hekate not*
> *awe-inspiringly beautiful?*

When I arose today at 6 a.m., my intention was to write of Hekate's epiphany. I was going to say that my research showed me that manifestations of Hekate, along with other gods and goddesses, are regularly preceded or simultaneously accompanied by cosmological and meteorological disruptions. Apollonius Rhodius documents Hekate's advent as heralded by an earthquake; "bellowings from the ground" immediately precede her epiphany.

Before I got as far as the actual research, I began writing freely and ended up writing about the earthquake, which I hadn't realized was going to be part of the Epiphany piece. In fact, when I finished writing, I was sorry I hadn't attended better to the business of recording my research. The next thing I heard on the radio was that there had been an earthquake, her epiphany, heralding her arrival in Palm Desert. A third thing absolutely connected with Hekate. The three-ness of the moment shook me. What synchronicity!

[Fig. 34]

GETTING
READY
FOR
HEKATE

Under Veil: Ghostly

Hekate, especially adept with ghosts, both brought and banned fear.[129]
        —James Hillman

[Fig. 35]

Witch's Sabbat: Hekate's Sabbatical

The Sabbat is a holy day set apart for building up the spiritual element in [ourselves].

—Philo of Alexandria, Jewish philosopher

I FOCUS ON HEKATE WITHOUT RETICENCE OR SHAME now that I have renounced the outer world's workaday spirit; I am burrowed into my cave communicating with very few for the time being. I have not designed this time, which feels strangely lonely; it has been given to me and in painful ways I wouldn't have asked for. But as it turns out, I am free, no bonds with agencies or institutions, no deadlines, no one else's ideas or prescriptions except Hekate's to follow in my writing.

You should know, however, that Hekate's Sabbat is not exactly the same as that of the 16th-century Kabbalists, that is, the Jewish mystics. They ran out to the fields chanting, "Come let us welcome the Shabbat Queen!" But they did not allow writing on the Sabbat. On Hekate's Sabbat, I have the best of both holy days. But, of course, every day can be Hekate's day. Maybe this will become a sabbatical year, or better yet, a sabbatical life!

In the existential sense, I am condemned to this freedom. Ironically, I'm finding that I like it, like tangling with the possibilities and being nose-to-nose with myself to face the issues of developing my creative impulse into a body of work, flesh in the world, something with psychic guts in it. I know that this is possible only through Hekate. Finally, I can tolerate not being distracted from my work with Hekate. I don't want to be distracted from my work with her; when I am, I become irritable like the witch that the world believes to be the whole of Hekate.

Witch's Sabbat. Hekate's Sabbatical. It's all the same as I stand over the cauldron of this work: stirring, stirring. Moving through each day, I feel her presence touch me, alive in me, but in a way I haven't felt before; I feel easier, less emotionally taut. I have become increasingly aware of this truth I'm living: Hekate is going to be with me wherever I go; she is in my ear whispering, in my eye pointing out remnants of her reality here and there.

Five years: I accept Hekate heartily into my life as a living reality. In me, she cannot be only a shard. She has grown from a small piece of my first image of her into the vast and profound being befitting a deity. She is no mere remnant. Grasping Hekate's essence in the world in both past and modern terms prompts me to think that all of my life has been a preparation for this time of consciously and deliberately creating a place for her to dwell: in this time, in this writing, in my body, in the bodies of all women and all men. This work, clearly, is an attempt to embody archetypal reality without being identified with it. This work is the learning process and moves beyond books; it illustrates the need and value of learning something as we live it. Clearly, it s urgent to trust living and what comes from living per se—that is, the art of living.

Feel the life? The burning, turning spirit of Hekate?

[Fig. 36]

Hekate Purifying (Hekate Purificata)

HERE WE ARE IN HEKATEAN TIME, FEELING OUR WAY. Imagine: The supper ritual, purification, and expiatory sacrifices are conducted at regular intervals on the house and household and on individuals. Though some part of the ceremonial takes place in and about the house, the remains of these rituals are left at the crossroads by worshippers, who retire "without looking back." Don't look back! The placing of the remains at the crossroads is particularly important in relation to the eggs and dogs used in house purification sacrifices. Each member of the family touches these beings to be offered. It is common for supplicants to rub against their bare skin the bodies of dead puppies sacrificed to Hekate to erase impurity.[130] This is how the dog, our oldest domesticated animal, acts as a scapegoat for the entire household.

House fumigation is an important detail of ritual. The censor, a baked clay pot, is used in the ceremony and then left at the crossroads, the only surviving object used in the sacrificial offering.

Unfortunately, these rituals have become confused with each other over time. Any interference with them or with the offerings to Hekate is considered sacrilegious and liable for punishment by us mere mortals. For example, one does not look back for fear that daemonic spirits will be angry if the worshipper appears to be looking at them. Some even believe that at the crossroads, Hekate fastens upon the guilty wretch who goes after her foul supper. Hekate is said to punish the poor creature with madness or some similar affliction of which she is supposed to be the primary cause.

Not surprisingly, superstitions exist about the crossroads and the events that occur there. Just to step on the crossroads, even accidentally, is considered dangerous! One passerby who chances to observe another feasting on garlic at the crossroads will go away, pour water over his head, and, summoning the priestesses, bid them to carry a puppy and a squill (a flowering plant used for rat poison and as a cardiac stimulant, expectorant, and diuretic!) for purification. And in much the same manner that people ate or wore garlic for health, eggs were eaten because they were thought to absorb impurities. Figs, thought to have magical properties because they are never struck by lightning, were worn as garlands around the necks of sorceresses who were also beaten with fig branches in purification rites. Finally, they were driven out of town as scapegoats.[131]

Of all the cults that have been passed down from ancient time, *Hekate's exhibits the most vitality*. Now that you get a sense of what it is to honor Hekate out of fear, you also need to know that she is deeply rooted in the hearts of the people who have participated in her cults. After the ritual is said and done, the truth is that the rich set down the meals every month for the benefit of the poor. This makes Hekate the goddess of leftovers, the poor, the wanderer, the bag lady, the homeless—doesn't it?

Can you imagine cooking for the homeless as an honoring of Hekate and as an expression to these Hekatean souls that they, too, are blessed with healthy, hearty food?

[Fig. 37]

I Dream of Hekate

I dream:

Other parts to this dream fell away.
All that is left is the image of a very old woman
wearing layer upon layer of black clothing:
some very delicate, some sheer, like chiffon;
some sturdy like wool, some strong but rich like velvet.
I'm amazed. The woman belongs to herself and is oddly
forceful —an elegant and dignified bag lady.

No doubt she is an image of Hekate!

Hekate's Suppers:
Cult of the Dead Ritual

"HEKATE'S SUPPERS" ARE THE OFFERINGS THAT FOLKS laid at the crossroads in honor of Hekate at the new moon—or its eve—of each month. These dinners were set with the purpose of placating the temperament of the underworld Hekate and her ghostly daemones, those souls who do not rest easy in their graves.

The new moon indicates Hekate's appearance from the depths of Hades. The 30th of the month, another day offered in service to the dead is also a day of sacrifice to Hekate. In Athens, the last three days of the month are sacred to the powers of the underworld and so are offered to Hekate and the

[Fig. 38]

Dead with offerings of libations. On the eve of the full moon, Hekate is remembered at the crossroads with a cake surrounded by lighted torches.

Le Menu:
- *loaf of grain*
- *sprat: a small marine food fish*
- *garlic*
- *mullet: a red-purpose fish whose name is related to melancholy*
- *sacrificial cake: the ingredients of which are not clear*
- *eggs*
- *cheese*

This bill of fare possesses virtue and associations commending them to Hekate and her crew. In ancient times, the cock, for example, heralded the sun and summoned ghosts to return to their places. For ancients, this is why eggs were so consistently associated with the cult of the dead. Garlic used as protection against vampires originated from their use at these services. The use of mullet is emblematic of religious conservatism. All of this food is meant to avert the easily aroused wrath of Hekate; her Callimachus called her "an epithet that expressed the worshippers' prayer that 'good digestion wait on appetite.'"[132]

Eugholine: Contented
      Easy
      Good-natured
      Popular

These are the epithets for Hekate that have been in hiding! Amazing grace, yes?

EI—

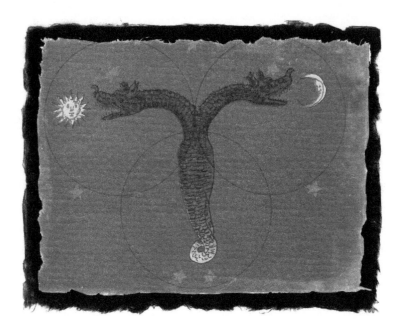

[Fig. 39]

EI —

The root of initiation: Janus-faced-the-divine witness of goings in and comings out, transits, transitiveness, seeing the beginning of the New Year. Roots in perish, in coitus, reconciling opposites, is a companion throughout the journey. The root "EI-" grows out of the realm of Hekate. Initiation begins with and is rooted in the realm of Hekate, telling our yearning souls that we must learn our safe, secure place, risk turmoil, make the crossing, and find out what lies beyond the threshold deep into uncharted landscape, into the cave of ourselves.

[Fig. 40]

Day 6 — The Initiation Mysteries at Eleusis: Witnessing Hekate

I AM *MYSTAI*, HERE TO WITNESS EVENTS, TO BATHE IN the mystery of darkness, to follow in the footsteps of the grieving goddess: not drama but divine presence that makes real the myth of Demeter and Persephone—and Hekate. Yes, she is here. Without her, there is no dark depth to the sacred trinity in our feminine experience. Quietly, listen in:

I will tell you little. I can say only that evening is given over to dromena, sacred enactments.

Then, deiknymena: *those things we show. The mystery of showing hiera carried in winnowing baskets.*

I cannot share the holy words of legomena: but only reveal these as a short and prayerful litany.

Women and men, we come to learn the great secret; we come to experience the great vision; we come to attain Epopteia: *We see the ineffable.*

And of Hekate? She lives between the moments when Demeter's motionless suffering and sorrow collide with her violent

*rage and Persephone's childish intoxication
fuses with her royal wifeliness. Hekate comes
up in the shadow of their vitality carrying the
torch of their reunion. But for Hekate,
Mother and Daughter might have been lost
to each other forever!*[133]

—Author's exhortation

Regarding men in the Eleusinian mysteries, the ancient voice that echoes forward from Eleusis tells us that men initiated into the mysteries along with women who each "became" the *Goddess*, not the god, so that they might rediscover and experience profoundly the nature of their feminine being. Only then could they free themselves from mother-possession of their girlish femininity; only then would they trust that they could find a ripened inner woman, the duality of mother and maiden.[134]

A dream:

*I am at a drycleaners near Beverly and
Vermont in Los Angeles, an area where a
great many Latino people live. I have an
attractive dress I want them to clean. I
believe I'm to wear it to some special event,
ceremony, or celebration. It's just a typical
cleaning establishment, yet they want to
charge me a ridiculous price for cleaning the
dress. I'm not sure the shop is even adequate
to do the task. My mother is "in" on this
errand, but only knows half of what is going
on. She doesn't know what it's really going to*

*cost to have the dress cleaned. I leave to go
to the Chinese cleaners near my house
instead. Somehow, I'm back in the Latino
cleaners, but the woman in charge is no
longer Chinese or Latina but Filipina; she
also wears black. I seem to be going
somewhere very special and want the dress
altered for the occasion. Not only do I leave
my black dress, but other items as well. I
rationalize the expense to myself by saying
that establishments that cater to
entertainment industry people always cost
more. My mother is indignant. I make some
movement towards her with a broom Kung-
Fu style. We settle the matter somehow, and
so I leave the clothes.*

This dream is to me a revealing description and
prelude to the initiation of the woman dreamer into
the deep, dark feminine mysteries. The images that
illuminate the psychic vestibule in which this
experience occurs are the act of cleaning/purifying,
the coming special event/celebration, the dark
women who (instead of the Asian woman) must
perform the cleaning rite, their dark dresses
corresponding to the initiate's own black ceremonial
robe, and the double sense of "altered." Most
important in this dream is the dreamer's conflict
about the initiation process. On one hand, she seems
excited, looking forward; on the other hand, she is
very concerned, searching for the right cleaners. She
fears that the one she's chosen may not be adequate
(and then the choice is taken from her as the Chinese

cleaner transfigures again into the Latin cleaner and with a Filipina attending her). Moreover, she's skeptical of the one she entrusts with her celebratory garb, fearful of being cheated.

To confirm the distinctly Hekatean nature of this dream, the dreamer with the broom (Hekate's horse) shows that she has the unbridled instinctive power of the horse on her side. In this display is a coming to terms, a new understanding that forms between the dreamer and cleaner that allows them to proceed. The woman will submit herself to the cleaning, the purging, or willing sloughing-off of whatever is unneeded in order to be initiated into the depths of the instinctual feminine mystery.

Another dream:

I start out in the mouth of some caves. I'm looking for something primitive which is meant to be seen there. . .ruins or art of some kind, but I'm not sure what. I don't find it right off. I go around and about in the caves and end up in some administrative buildings attached to the caves. I watch others going to and fro; I wander a bit. (Scene change.) I'm going through a toll plaza; the attendant hands me change, a $5 bill. I'm almost sure that it's counterfeit. I'm moving through quickly so I don't take the time to say anything. I end up back at the cave and try to go in. People there notice that the bill is

bogus and would have apprehended me
except that I more or less acknowledge it and
tell them about the toll plaza. I am allowed
to pass. I continue my search with a greater
sense of direction (more a feeling of
determination to go ahead undeterred than
of physically mapping my way).

[Fig. 41]

Lily and Carol talking:
Hekate's Eros

WHENEVER MY COLLEAGUE SUSAN AND I GET TOGETHER for lunch, cappuccino, or a walk, soon enough during the conversation we begin to speak from other parts of ourselves than our heads. Though generally silent about the shift, we are each aware of the moment when this happens. When it does, we have two other names, "Lily" and "Carol," which surface from the etymological underbellies of our respective given names. Cats also have these underbelly names; in fact, all cats have one name that no one knows, or so the story goes. Maybe this occurs because Bastet, the ancient Egyptian cat goddess, rules the world "Under-." The moment Susan and I become "Lily" and "Carol," we connect by some mysterious means with our cat natures and can venture into the land where Bastet rules: deeply into matters of the psyche, the realm of Hekate.

One day we met at Chloe's for lunch and as usual we filled each other in on the crucial happenings of the moment. When it was my turn, I told Lily that the burning question in my life centered on the nature of my experience of Hekate, barely aflame yet abiding in the shadow of Eros, the Greek god of relationship. I added that it was intuitively clear to me that revealing shadow—an intangible, unseen potential with a felt presence—could likely create eros (relatedness). By extension, revealing Hekate could create eros. I told her, as I noted earlier in my writing that, innately, I knew for certain the truth of this idea. We agreed that proof could not be made by the usual empirical evidence or deductive reasoning. However, I am aware of enough tales from others and from my own life to confirm this sense of Hekate.

I considered, especially, the relationship between the deities, Eros and Hekate, and envisioned Eros' arrow, which at first I mistook for Hekate. Then I saw her in an image as the *unseen force* propelling the arrow to its target, a revelation.

Since that day of destiny, when Hektate rose up from the book stack, I have felt certain of her revelatory moments—that is, when she shows me something that represents her in the modern world. A quality in these epiphanies is irrefutable. From these, I trust her as the force of connection that rests in shadow waiting for the moment of entry, as if out of the wings onto a stage. I have felt her force ongoing, not spiritualized or transcendent, not the eros aspect that society collectively understands as the totality of eros but the chthonic—Underworld—quality of Hekate's nature, which is also erotic. I know this quality as the opposite and equal complement to spiritual transcendence that is our legacy from the courtly love of the Renaissance.

Lily and I sat rapt in Hekatean reality, not talking about her as much as experiencing her by living through the nature of experience itself that arose from *telling* the Psyche and Eros tale. Lily saw Psyche in a kind of Underworld tableau, a fresco-like portrayal; she stood in that space "beside." As if witnessing her vision, I said, "Yes, I find Hekate constantly in that place; she dwells engaged and maybe engaging the space *between* and *among* figures. I know her as ever-present, an essential partner—not demanding or even wanting the spotlight, but there to be called on, to step in, to invisibly conjoin or carry forward what seemingly cannot be done otherwise." I noted that in Greek art, she is most often portrayed in this position of "between-ness," a nexus in white space.

Hekate in the tableau: What has she to do with Psyche's journey? Robert Graves tells us that Hekate and Perephone stood for the pre-Hellenic hope of regeneration. Could the invisible Hekate along with Persephone be the unspoken aids of Psyche in her struggle to satisfy the irrepressible rage of Mother Aphrodite, from another ancient tale of a daughter's efforts to grow into womanhood? Homer reminds me that in the aftermath of Persephone's abduction by Hades, Hekate actually leads and follows Persephone, guiding and protecting her.

All young psyches, female or male, for want of eros, are also shadowed by Hekate. Hekate is the force, the deep dark experience of yearning and desperation that thrusts forward unexpectedly from nowhere that reaches beyond itself and risks all: From the shadow, it is Hekate's hand guiding Psyche as she opens the divine beauty box of Persephone. Did you know that in ancient times, Persephone and Hekate were often taken for each other? When Psyche reaches for Persephone, she reaches also for Hekate; she reaches not only for eternal youthful beauty but also for dark instinctual femininity that gives her to herself in whole womanliness and in womanly wholeness. Even in deathly sleep, Psyche exudes that Underworld queenly appeal irresistible to the gods. Eros can't resist! Without recognizing the sacredness of such beauty, sexuality comes easily perverted and pornographic. The nature of sexual addiction arises from such submerged sanctity of our sexual nature. Compulsively, we repeat the search unaware of what we are really looking for, unconscious of our true need or that we have found what we truly need.

BETWEEN

Definition: In or through the position or interval
                separating.
                Intermediate to, as in quantity,
                amount, or degree; space or time.
                Connecting spatially by the combined
                effort or effect of.
                As measured against.
                Often used to express a reciprocal
                relationship as in choosing between
                2 entities

Dwo- etymology: *Duwo* is variant form. Two (from
the German *twa*, which share roots with the number
12, the most complete number in ancient Greek
thinking).
Also *dwi*, which leads to twilight.
Also *dekm; one* can't speak of these numbers
without evoking Hekate for *dekm,* which is the root
of Hekate's hundreds, her many formed-ness.[135]

                —*American Heritage Dictionary*

Clearly, the land *between* is the realm of Hekate.

WOE-
IS-
ME,
HEKATE

Hekate, Body #9: 1988

woman-fingers of Jin Shin. Penetrate
pulses find grief in wrists

crossroads on fire
Hekate in my body.
hold these points
touch-in-me throbs
at number nine, under my wing
place of transitions,
twilight between here and there
at number ten, underside of the blade,
cuts through folds of voice-blood
cycling,
to twelve,
where heart's clutching hands 'round my neck,
scream "Submit!"
call it completion if you will
thirteen, lungs, home of grief,
where chaos sweats form.
* Hekate*
at home in my body, howling dog
of pain
she waits for me
hold ache two fingers
So lightly
touch dark morning of new moon
so slowly it waxes into fullness

I do this every day for one year.

—Shira Marin

[Fig. 42]

Breaking Hekate: Reflections on a Fracturing Image of Hekate

I LOOK FORWARD TO "WRITING DAY," BUT THEN TODAY arrived, and my task is difficult: I feel low, am distracted but fend off most of what detains me. Still, I cannot shake this feeling.

Is it that your message is often a tale of woe? You are the messenger of grief; you are the potency of brokenness, of sorrow incarnate. In my attempt to convey your nature, how much is my feeling connected with yours? How much of the feeling of shattered power belongs to my sympathy with you, my living out your reality? Is this experience for the world to know? And if it is not, what of you? What will happen to the restoration of your wholeness? I will not let go of the pieces, the shards of you.

Did you feel a failure as the Great Mother when your sons and, finally, your daughters began to turn on you, to find you controlling and despicable— when your expressions of love came to be seen as smothering and emasculating of men, these same men to whom you gave support in battle, in court, on the land?

I have been experiencing your darkness again, your hiddenness, as it was forced down and out of sight ages ago by the tumescent thrust of patriarchal consciousness. Am I experiencing your frustration, their forgetfulness, their unconscious depotentiation of you who have given so bountifully to them, to all those who would depose you? The development of the human ego became unable to tolerate its own darkness and limitations, its own diffuse light, its own unknowing-ness; we colored you evil and cast you out. So long ago, so unconsciously, we cast you out.

You cannot return without revealing these humiliations: of disregard, of exclusion, of forgotten-ness, of shame. In delving into your nature, I discover my own inner experiences and tremble with the question, "What must it be to suffer the humiliation of a goddess, the divine degradation?" Hekate, you are the archetypal image of denounced being: of the logic of feeling, of irrefutable instinctual knowing, of intuitive vision, of tenderness, of acceptance of life just as it presents itself. Hekate, present yourself fully and be our saving grace.

Hekate Returns: 1990

THEY HAD NO WAY OF KNOWING I'D JUST COME UP
from down under. No, not that Down Under, but
Tartarus. Clearly, they had no idea what it might be
like to stand in Italian soil at the threshold of
Avernus midway between there and eternity, having
just arrived slightly rumpled from the Other Side,
Naples lying before me. I'd been watching it grow
over the years, but standing there, I hardly
recognized the place. This was not the metropolis of
the old days. I dusted myself off and assumed my
usual carriage. Unlike before, no one recognized me.
But then I had left my dog at home, no torches or
snakes. There were not shrines or temples to remind
anyone. People looked at me like I was dressed
funny. I looked around and realized women weren't
wearing chitons anymore, although sandals still
seemed to be popular.

I thought I was expected; the word had gotten
out that I was coming. I heard that a lot of women
had been preparing the way in the last five years, so
when I finally arrived at the meeting, I had a sense
that there was going to be someplace to settle in.

As I began to talk with people, I realized that
we hardly spoke the same language anymore.
Awkward. I was not who they anticipated. I feared
that I had been away too long and that these people
had strayed far from the well that feeds the tree of
life, that slakes the fruit of us, and feeds our souls.

Krataiis Hekate: Strong

IN HEKATE'S DEMISE, WE CAN SEE THE ARCHETYPE OF "falling to pieces." Often we talk of falling apart, falling to pieces. We hear this comment made about women but believe it is because of weakness as opposed to coming through the archetypal feminine nature of Hekate. In times of stress, many of us want to keep to the straight and narrow path, to an untampered masculine sense of life that somehow keeps our feeling life in check. We don't have to feel the full importance of the moment or the feelings hidden behind the façade. It becomes habit to pretend that all's well. The habit has us! It is only when we allow for Hekate's value to become real in us that we have the chance to find the deepest truth of our feelings; we have to risk allowing the whole to break into pieces to see what will happen then. When we don't want to risk falling to pieces, we don't want to see or experience what lies inside, and sometimes there may be a valid reason one would not want to pursue this path. Most often, I have found that we are more afraid of our anxious spinning about what might happen than what actually occurs from taking such a chance. In the truth of my experience, most conflict and most incapacity to transit psychological impasse involve a failure of imagination and a failure to listen in the way Lee Glickstein describes as Luminous Listening. Luminous listening not only occurs through the ears but also in the eyes and heart. It expresses the connectedness of our human experience, of all things that inhabit the earth. It is a listening that grounds and stabilizes us in our wholeness. If we listen in this way, we hear the soul's yearning to express itself. It is the longing of the Hekatean Feminine Principle to be felt and heard. She is calling us back to our deepest instinctual ground, the one out of which she grows, flowers, and manifests our innate goodness even in our mistakes. She speaks with the voice of the Friend, the one who companions us with compassion and encourages us, lending guidance and care in life's journey.[136]

Come along, let's listen to the Friend and traverse the plain of not-knowing.

[Fig. 43]

Under Where: What Jesus Said

ONE DAY, I SAT IN FRONT OF THE FIRE ALL DAY TENDING logs of "iffy" maturity. I penned "FAILURE" in huge letters across an art pad. In vivid colors, at least: beet red, pumpkin orange, dirt brown. Furious earth; little or no depression. The claws of failure ripped into the bloody flesh of my soul. I recalled trying to read *The Music of Failure*—the dirge of failure then.[137] I couldn't help wondering if those who read these pages will wrestle with pitiful confusion, internally thrashing about. Is there anything like the pangs of failure?

I hadn't learned how to fail successfully at all. I'm getting the hang of it now; only getting hanged by it now, not so long, not as often. Finally, I realize how much practice it takes to grasp the nature and value of failure, and what failing can teach.

Failing feels like hell, Hell feels like Hekate: Hekate, driven-out-witch to be rejected; the one no one wants. The failed woman. The failed feminine. That's what happened to her. (And consequently to us!) *They* broke and banished her. Did she fail them, or they her?

Either way, for what purpose is all of this? What does it serve? Hekate's failure, Hekate failed, my own sense of failing, not being able to find the words, feeling failed; how am I tied to Hekate in suffering failure? What am I to grasp from this canon of sorrow? I read a little; not much gets done. I remember something Russ Lockhart said in *Psyche*

Speaks, which he applied to the psyche and that also applies to Hekate, Mother of the wordless, Mother of sorrow, Mother of the homeless soul:

> . . .*it's not women only who are suffering in our time, not even the feminine only; psyche is victim. Psyche itself in need of nursing. And I thought that madness must nourish psyche because in our enormous capacity to deny the imaginative reality that is psyche, to reserve psyche only to the material world we call reality, that denied and rejected psyche will in fact materialize right before our very eyes. Who can deny the reality of the psyche when one walks our streets today? It is visible, present, materialized in the behavior and bodies and the voices we try not to see, try not to hear. Psyche has become real in this way because we fail in so many ways to grant psyche reality. If we can't find food for psyche, psyche will feed on madness, nurse on madness.*[138]

These words remind me that Hekate has become real in the way we now know her for the same reasons. She, like the psyche, feeds on the madness of being ignored and forgotten—that is, being unrelated to. This lack of relatedness began long ago, perhaps even before the ancient Chaldeans considered Hekate and psyche to be one and the same. Maybe they were a small enclave who grasped the nature of the Hekatean psyche and valued it highly. But at the same time, ego consciousness developed and patrilineal lines formed. Little by little, both the psyche and Hekate were moved into darkness and the isolation that comes with darkness and the rage that comes with loneliness and the desire to strike back at those who neglect and forget. Strange to think of the nurse goddess in need, herself, of nursing. The psyche is always there to feed us if we seek to engage her. Was I failing to engage psyche, to implore the one who made this journey possible in the first place?

The most important thing I have learned about failing is that it is grounding. In fact, it is under-grounding: Failing pulls me into the roots of anger, angry words, cross words, ritualized words muttered in the shadow of loss. There I was at the "crosswords: of road and shadow—a cursed slip evokes Hekate! I meant "at the crossroads of word and shadow again," referring to my fallow field of words. Either way, Hekate appeared. There's no forgetting that she presides over our dark nature, the shadow which contains the crude and undeveloped Self as well as the hidden golden one, and like the shadow she is always a step ahead or a step behind. Hekate is nothing less than the goddess of the archetype of failure!

Ahead. Behind. The sense of "having a lead" and "trailing" reminds me to look for her again and there she is, right before my eyes, in the Sunday *San Francisco Examiner* a "female gumshoe" article about women mystery writers—an Hekatean line of work if ever there were one (as either the writer or the gumshoe herself). Gumshoes are forever looking for the hidden, the seemingly nonexistent, the invisible.

Perhaps all the talk of following clues launched me into *Leaping Poetry,* by Robert Bly. In this book, Bly writes about the need for and value of quick associations in making good poems, how we need to leap into the unconscious psyche for this to happen or otherwise we end up along the same track of associations time and again. But the issue of sameness is really the issue of needing to go Under. Going Under lands us in chthonic earth, one of Hekate's three domains.

The movement down, to things that bring me down, are my mother's hospitalized heart to recent damnable dreams and disappointments; I was on the verge of deciding that I had no path, at least not one that included Hekate. But a saying from Jesus in the *Gnostic Gospel of Thomas* was on my tail all day yesterday:

> *If you bring forth what is within you,*
> *what you bring forth will save you.*
> *If you do not bring forth what is within you,*
> *what you do not bring forth will destroy you.*

Another movement in and down. This project is surely a form of bringing out what creative impulse lives in me, my experience of Hekate who seemingly wants to come openly into modern times. I, too, want to come into modern times: to follow her, bring her, companion her. Her myth, long forgotten, demands of me to speak Hekate's voice loud and clear into our modern times. I have, like Hekate, a difficult time coming forth. I am unduly attached to anonymity for one who used to spend so much time in the necessarily exhibitionistic career of actress/songstress. But the work of psychologist-writer creates the most outstanding persona of all for one who would rather remain unseen. Concealment as persona is one of the best hiding places of all. But the truth of my hiding, like Hekate's, involves shame: that primitive sense that one ought to be visible but not really seen and certainly not heard.

With the rise of the aggressive masculine, Zeus and Olympiad pushed themselves from the Greek chorus onto center stage, front line. So, concealment is everything for Hekate as the goddess of darkness and of all things driven underground. Were we to appreciate Hekate's being, instead of denouncing Hekate, we would celebrate all attributes at Hekate's major festival in Autumn, the season of life retreating into darkness. The beauty of Hekate at this time is in the burst of color vibrating the affirmation of life and the promise of death followed silently with an act of faith in Spring renewal, the Resurrection as Christians commemorate it. But then, the Christians seized their idea from the woman-centered cults of ancient times and, specifically, from the death-rebirth cyclical nature that is Hekate's! So, Jesus and egg, as both death and life symbols, and the rabbit, standing for the multiplication of new life, tie death to life: concealment to bursting forth. Renewal is the act of bringing forth again. Jesus, in his gnostic moment, was clearly the emissary of Hekate. The narrative that is Jesus expresses the ultimate instinctual knowing, the ultimate in active compassion for himself and others that brings new life.

The supposed failure of Jesus was no less than redemption. Many have called Jesus Christ's work and his being a folly and a sham. But I have no doubt that when I have worked resolutely to stop bringing forth altogether this work with Hekate, my life has taken wrong turns. In the psyche's terms, in Hekate's terms, in Jesus' terms, I have failed. Sometimes we have to take what seem to be wrong turns, to fail to find our right way. Failing often feels fiercely painful. But what we learn on these forays, intentional or otherwise, informs us in ways we couldn't have imagined. Consider that Hekate is leading us through the byways of the Underworld, as she did with Persephone; we cannot find our way through without her. We need this journey with Hekate to come to the inner truth of our being, to find our way up from under, to burst through the hard-packed earth into the new form that has rooted in our inner darkness and must express the new potential from souls in hiding from the world.

Some paths are far more difficult to treat—they are physically and emotionally treacherous—and one wonders whether survival is possible, nothing less than the labors of Psyche or those of Hercules. Such labors have occurred by divine decree in both ancient and modern times. I can't think of this work in any other way. So, thankfully, nothing lived, even loss, need be considered a waste or devalued as a learning or the spur to becoming, particularly depending on how one relates to what one discovers. Or so experience has taught me. Pollyanna? Only to those who refuse to consider the interconnectedness of life and possible unseen alien hands that hold an individual—striving, intentionally or not, toward constellated wholeness. The invisible hands that reach out to me belong to Hekate, guiding my way through momentary failure en route to joyful success. Unlike me, she never forgets that the two are the same and prompts me to keep my commitment, the act that engenders renewal. Spoken or silent, commitment is everything. A quote of Goethe's came to me:

> *Until one is committed, there is hesitancy, the chance to draw back, always ineffectiveness. Concerning all acts of initiative (and creation), there is one elementary truth the ignorance of which kills countless ideas and splendid plans: That moment one definitely commits oneself, then Providence moves, too. All sorts of things occur to help one that would never otherwise have occurred. A whole stream of events issues from the decision, raising in one's favor all manner of unforeseen incidents and meetings and material assistance, which no man would have dreamed would have come his way. Whatever you can, or dream you can, begin it. Boldness has genius, power, and magic in it. Begin it now.*[139]

Failure and commitment go together. In the shadow of failure is the renewal of commitment to the stretch of unknown life beyond what we see. There: At the crossroads, Hekate turns the spiral in the roiling cauldron of unseen images until, from its depths, the right one reveals itself and speaks to us.

> *In all art derived from the Great Mother*
> *mysteries,*
> *the leap into the unknown part of the mind*
> *lies in*
> *the very center of the work.*[140]
> —Robert Bly

Note: *We* are the art derived from the great mother, Hekate: Meditate on this. Let Hekate fill the open space in your being. She waits in your darkness to embrace your love, your yearning heart, and longing soul. Put her at the center now. Can you feel the difference? Feel the difference!

November 19th , 5:45 a.m. Foggy wraiths again. I woke thinking this morning—after last night's dream, which I can't wholly remember—that it's wrong-headed to think that Hekate and I can't finish our work. We are in labor: Hekate, Midwife-nurse and Foster Mother. The Goddess Mother will bear this labor to birth, to Hekate's own rebirth.

> *. . . Words strain, crack and sometimes break,*
> *under the burden, under the tension, slip,*
> *slide, perish,   decay with imprecision,*
> *will not stay in place, will not stay still.*
> *Shrieking voices*
> *Scolding, mocking, or merely chattering,*
> *Always assail them.*
> *The Word in the desert is most attached by*
> *voices of temptation,*

The crying shadow in the funeral dance,
The lament of the disconsolate chimera[141]

—T. S. Eliot

Deliver imagination. Hekate belongs to this world, the Three in the One: New-born Mother, Godmother teetering over what place is hers, sends me into Mother Demeter's wandering depression: hiding bounty under a sackcloth mantle, using sacred power to create barrenness over bounty. The loss of my connection to my own divine child is at stake.

Golden daughter Persephone can be destroyed by staying in the Demetrian state of mind. But not only that. The loss of Hekate also is at stake. The renewal of her far-reaching femininity, which includes not only the child aspect but also Hekate, the Foster Mother. When we are psychically abducted into the "mist darkness" of the Underworld, Hekate is our mother who listens and hears us; when no one else can, with her torch alight, she leads the way. In the Homeric hymn, only the Sun and Hekate, "alone in her tenderness. . .from her cave," heard the daughter who "screamed in a shrill voice calling for Zeus, her supreme and powerful father."[142] It was Hekate who brought about the reunion between Persephone and her mother Demeter.

These myths guide me to that same point: Hekate, crowned with bright headband, is the feminine link which re-joins my inner and outer worlds, restoring to my own inner child the joy of being connected fully with the world in the way she desires—to be alive in the immediacy of the moment that includes both realms.

Feeling at home above and below, Persephone returns to her mother in the upper world, to find that from then on, Hekate both precedes and follows her, accompanying and guiding her, veiled in shadow but still with bright headband, always there. As Hekate draws me into the world through this work, too comes back into the world. My project is to follow her, to attend the birth of this piece, not to allow anything to abort it. Urging Hekate into the open world is a care, which has been given to me. As I tried to let go of the world again, I realized this very early morning that it is impossible. By the light of Hekate's headband and torch, the only way is *through* the agonizing darkness.

The difference: The more I allow Hekate to be at the center of my being, to be with my unknown but her fruitful darkness, the more confident and trusting I feel along the path of illuminating my ancient mother in our new postmodern world.

Come along: Discover your own verdant, fruitful darkness: Hekate!

You'll see the woman
Hanging upside down
Her features covered by her fallen gown
. . .I've seen the future, baby, it
is murder.[143]

—Leonard Cohen

[Fig. 44]

3 Women Hanging

A woman dreams:

I go to a museum and see many exhibits presented by Amnesty International. These depict scenes of torture as a means of awakening us to the reality of hostages in the world today. I come to the last exhibit and see three women hanging, swinging slowly back and forth. One sways and turns to reveal not an unknown face but my face. I am startled but see the truth in this.

HEKATE, I SAW YOU BEFORE I KNEW OF MAIDEN sacrifice made in your honor. It was not only the death imagery, not only your triple nature and that they were women, not only that Amnesty International begged for freedom from oppression. It was something more, greater than all of these parts. You speak to this woman as one of your daughters. Your symbolic death heralds renewal in this daughter. Months later, your truth reappeared.

I read from an ancient manuscript:

A hanged woman becomes Hekate.[144]

—Callimachus

Maiden sacrifice stands in contrast, and provides a balance, to the main sacrifice that supplies the food. It is a ritual of giving in order to get. During [this preliminary

sacrifice] . . .there is an anticipatory self-denial which consequently requires forms of destruction-submerging in water, hanging from trees.[145]
—William Burkhert

Hekate, archetype of the sacrifice of feminine nature in this patriarchal world that has arisen out of your demise, we are doomed if sacrifice of our animal bodies continues. Will we only stop sacrificing ourselves when we stop sacrificing you? Without your rebirth, can we truly be reborn?

Definitely: We will *only* shift the murderous aspects of the patriarchy when you, your being in the world, is fully embraced—seen, heard, and held in our hearts, known as the radiance of our souls. You will be known as the blessing of our instinctive knowing, the deep, natural intelligence we have shunned for millennia. But little by little, you are returning, and I walk the path of you, the journey of your destiny and mine.

Salgado Re-members Hekate

1. Hekate,
2. Su,
3. Salgado,
4. & I

NUMBERED PARAGRAPHS. NOT HEADINGS. NOT ARBITRARY. But subjectively logical, as in the logic of truth. My friend Susan-as-poet is the only person I've ever seen who pictorializes this particular thinking pattern, which I had thought might be my private mental form. This shared privacy, this unspoken structure now made public, shocked me when I first saw it: her newly written piece. When I asked S. about the form of her essay on the world of photographer Sebastiao Salgado, she said simply that she had to tell the truth just as it presented itself to her in her body. Yes: that instinctive truth that will not let go. Salgado's vision of bodies starving, of human beings starving. And Susan's essay embracing the yearning hunger with simplicity, simply being there. Holding. Susan's essay: a container for the uncontainable feeling, the urgent telling, the ineffable pain.

That truth of her body became her body of work. Her form: How often does one consider the need to tell the truth in form! As if her skin were transparent, the news of Susan's fact and fiction woven into the wholeness of her. They are separated by their forms and yet are inseparable in the same way that, in our bodies, they are inseparable—in the same way that outer and inner realities are inseparable if one is going to tell the whole truth.

Immediately, I recognize Hekate in this kind of truth-telling within which the linkage between the two worlds is so tightly fit that these realms of experience are ineluctably *of* each other. Susan-of-Salgado-of-Hekate-and-of-me as observer. Susan-writing-of-Salgado-shooting. My seeing Salgado shooting and Susan writing: We all witness Hekate's message of grief. We are "of" Hekate in bearing witness to and partaking of Hekate's profound vision, of Hekate's image.

When I say "of," we participate in Hekate's paradox, which aligns us with the linguistic push and pull of the definitions from the *American Heritage Dictionary.* Look here:

> *Derived or coming from*
> *originating at or from*
> *caused by*
> *resulting from*
> *away from*
> *at a distance from*
> *relieved from*
> *from the total or group comprising*
> *composed or made from*
> *associated with or adhering to*
> *belonging or connected to*
> *possessing or having*
> *containing or carrying*
> *specified as*
> *named or called*
> *centering upon*
> *directed toward*

produced by
issuing from
characterized or identified by
concerning
with reference to
about
set aside for
taken up by
before
until
during or on

Etymology: spo-: off, away, away from, ebb, low tide, behind, after, again, awkward. Evening, even, next to.

What is the real, that is, Hekatean imaginal hinge between the root and the word?

Salgado's photographs:

derived from her
originated with her
were caused by her
resulted from her
unable to be taken away from[her]
not seen at a distance from [her]
not to be relieved from the truth of the total
moment of Hekate's grief
that belongs to and comprises her reality
that possesses us when we don't re-member
when we lose our sense of body
the body of truth that is Hekate
which is fostered by her

even as she fosters children
these children Salgado brings to her
Scrawny and bloated beside their withered
mothers and fathers
or all alone
a dog wanders over hillocks of graves sniffing
the dead
as if they would feed her
life without sustenance
life without
Hekate.

I doubt I could feel more grief-stricken by another's vision or the experience of life's wrenching truth—I cannot say "art"—than I felt during Salgado's exhibit. Stunned into silence, I was propelled from piece to piece by the inexplicable energy of this man who had the courage to become so extremely intimate with the pain of strangers and to so boldly offer it to the rest of us. What fostered this nerve? Not the art of suffering, not the exploitation of so many. Was it empathy for them or a challenge to our denial of the condition of excruciating sorrow? Was he overcome and unable to hold inside the intensity of this archetypal grief?

Gravity

Grief lies close to the roots of laughter.
Both love the cabin open to the traveler,
the ocean apple wrapped in its own leaves.
How can I be close to you if I am not sad?
There is a gladness in the not-caring of
the bear's cabin; and the gravity
that makes the stone laugh down the mountain.
The animal pads where no one walks.[146]

—Robert Bly

[Fig. 45]

On Assateague Island

November evening
Makes dusky
The dunes,
Gray sand
Deepens
And goes farther away.
I seldom speak
My grief,
I think it under
The water,
Turn it over
And over.
Herds of wild ponies
Leave hoofmarks
Up and down
This long
Forty mile island.
Some people respect
Only light
Streaming in
From distant stars.
I grieve
In Milky Ways
And Speak
In single stars.
I keep this grief
To myself.
My words
Are a single
Horse,
With low belly,
Alone[147]

—Robert Bly

Salgado Later On

Life is a secret buried under the garbage. That's what Sabastiao Salgado's photographs tell us. He [shows]us what is seen but unnoticed.[148]

Is it strange and significant; is it stunning that a couple of years after writing that Salgado remembers Hekate? I am color copying William Blake's painting of Hekate when an unknown man steps up beside me and plunks down a card with Salgado's name emblazoned on it. The man wants to duplicate the card as Salgado is to give an appearance and slide commentary in 10 days. Since I had written the Salgado piece two years prior, his name and work had not appeared even once. It's not just that I'm duplicating the Hekate painting. The greater point is embodied in the obvious living connection between Salgado's reality and Hekate's. Eduardo Galeano, the Uruguaryan journalist and author, notices this as I do when he says:

Salgado shows corpses with dignity and this is the source of their ineffable beauty.

This is Hekate's beauty, that Underworld beauty, which also belongs to Persephone and dwells in the shadow of Aphrodite.

> *Joy & Woe are woven fine, A*
> *Clothing for the Soul Divine*
> *Under every grief & pine*
> *Runs a joy with silken twine.*[149]

—William Blake

RE-
NEWING

*Is that scarecrow with its arms thrown open
a woman?*
                              —Edward Galeano

Hekate is waiting to embrace you. Will you
embrace her?

Hoc est enis corpus tuum: Body of Hekate, Amen!

WHEN ALLEGED CIVILIZATION SPLIT MIND AND BODY,
". . .the instinctive body was seen as a threat because
it represented the 'lower' animal aspects of human
nature. As the life of the body was suppressed, so,
too, was the receptive Feminine Principle. As clarity,
objectivity, and differentiation were developed and
given highest value, the Moon Goddess, who seeks
wholeness and completion, was sacrificed. Both the
body and [the feminine Self] were relegated to the
underworld, along with all that is despised and
rejected."[150]

In praise of you, Hekate, I raise your body
out of the underworld, the
root of you out of chthonic earth.
And aching from the birth of you, I
cast your fortune over into the arms of your
most holy Self.
You are your own:
Fate—even as you are my Destiny.

—Shira Marin, 1990

Even with the limitations of our fate, we can turn toward our destiny. Hekate will lead us there; I'm sure of it! Come along; allow your body, and its beauty, no matter its form, the full measure of your Love.

[Fig. 46]

A Thought at Winter Solstice

SOMEONE SAID RECENTLY THAT WHEN THE THRESHOLD
of renewal is missing, great sorrow comes as it did
when mother Demeter grieved the loss of sweet
daughter Persephone. But Hekate is the threshold of
renewal. So when Hekate comes, she makes real the
possibility of reunion of Demeter and Persephone as
she did in the myth.

Today, the sightings around the world of
Mother Mary's weeping recall Demeter's sorrow. She
cries a vast but silent despair to show us the true
depth of suffering that can precede renewal. She
shows us her longing to embrace us and to be
embraced by us all. She is a Mother for us all and
for all time. And sheltered amid those dark tears and
within that willing embrace is a small insistent flame
that kindles the fire of renewal, that returns a
daughter Persephone to her mother Demeter and,
together, they return the cycle to its ancient source:
Hekate.

Let Hekate reunite instinctual feminine being in
us—man and woman. Let us dignify our feminine
receptivity; let Hekate weave again the life of the
virgin with the whore, Father god with the pimp. Let
us be led by merging the split-off truth of our being.

[Fig. 47]

Poem for 7 December, 1987

lion and lamb
see the colors
the merest tint of blood
this pain-ting is of blood
only brown read this
soul
place of many colors
heart pouring out from the marshy
glade between these thighs
it pulses and hums with the
drone of Woman in time

there
One
lion and lamb

VISIONS OF
HEKATE
IN CLINIC
AND
DREAM

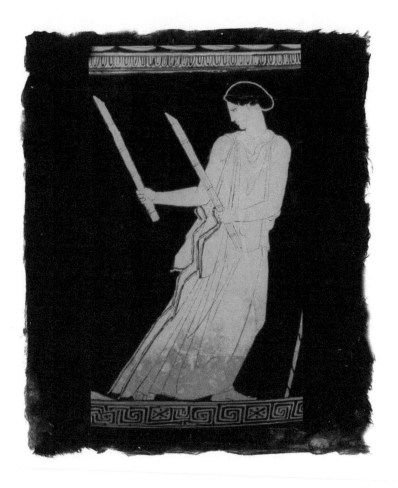

[Fig. 48]

Imagination is...

Imagination is the way we expand our vision.[151]
—Verena Kast

> *Dionysus wine and visionary possibilities:*
> *"The gift of prophecy had never been foreign*
> *to the Greek goddesses. During the*
> *Dionysian celebration, visions were*
> *formulated into words and then performed*
> *as tragedy. Thus, the gift of prophecy was*
> *very close to the art of poetry. . . The*
> *visionary state was entered into by*
> *undertaking the following activities: the*
> *drinking of wine, joining hands to create a*
> *mystic circle, a vessel capable of receiving*
> *divine inspiration, luring and invoking*
> *Dionysus. I'm not sure that we would be so*
> *comfortable calling god in this matter;*
> *perhaps we would like to but do not dare.*[152]

I'm not sure to whom Dr. Kast is referring here because experience tells me something different, but I was touched to see that even though she holds this view, she notes that our:

> . . .*unconscious longing for inspiration and*
> *ecstasy may well be characteristic of our age.*
> *We should at least permit ourselves these*
> *longings, even if we are no longer open to*

ecstasy itself. To be taken hold of by [divine nature] means to be possessed and to permit oneself to be possessed. . .the more defined the ego boundaries are, the greater their permeability.[153]

Yes, then we are safe as we call to take hold of and be taken hold of by Hekate, to heal the split between the Dionysian maenad and the demure maiden.

I dream again:

I seem to be standing on the brink of one side, the edge of a split; I'm being told something special and become filled with the sense that I won't fall. I must write down the vision as it is parallel to the dream!

I implore Hekate to heal the split. She tells me that I will not fall into the chasm of one-sidedness. I have found a bridge to hold the sphere of human being: body and spirit—Hekate.

[Fig. 49]

Angelos Hekate

Everywhere appearance and vision came, as it were, together in the object; in every one of them a whole inner world was exhibited, as though an angel, in whom space was included, were blind and looking into himself. This world, regarded no longer from the human point of view, but as it is within the angel, is perhaps my real task, one, at any rate, in which all my previous would converge.[154]

—Rainer Maria Rilke

Charle Olson, Robert Duncan, and Alan Ginsberg & Hekate— in Conversation

> *The greatest Angel known to man in the Greek system is Hekate; and I could prove it—I could read to you. . .which ought to forever put an end to this use of her as the frightful goddess, the goddess of fear, which is one of the damndest clichés we have, really. . .But, in fact, she is the great "angel" of her father; she does the real stuff. Whenever a real thing has to be done, she's sent to do it.*[155]

FOR YEARS, I HAVE SEEN HEKATE IN THE SHADOW OF the Christian archangel Michael. Look at what Charles Olson says about Hekate in a conversation published posthumously in the 1993 journal, *Sulfur*:

> *It's an amazing fact that Hekate was really. . .in our system, like Michael, the archangel. She's the archangel, early, look: a woman archangel. And, you know, she became, in some curious dumb problem of fear and fright, this monster. But she's no monster.*[156]

> —Charles Olson

So, it appears that in our fear we betrayed a truth of our nature, our instinctive knowing self. Instead of receiving her, instead of taking in her message of her truly angelic protective nature, of helping us to live fully and authentically, that is, in keeping with our deepest needs and desires, we rejected Hekate. In rejecting Hekate, we rejected the deepest truth of our being. It is from our *being* truth that we would understand our real and true priorities and engage with them naturally. Consider: What would happen if we dropped our fear long enough to embrace Hekate? I have—come try it. See what happens!

Himma: a Light Shadowing Eros

JAMES HILLMAN ILLUMINATES MY DAILY LIFE WITH
Hekate when in *The Thought of the Heart* he says,
"The power of the imagination is without doubt
[of the same nature] as soul." Read: essentially of
the same stuff as Hekate. The power, he notes,
describes the Sufi concept, "Himma," the rhetorical
imaginative power which, like the "enthymesis" of
the Greeks, "signifies the act of meditating,
conceiving, imagining, projecting, ardently desiring
. . .of having [something] present which is vital
force, heart, soul intention, thought, desire. . ." (all
that is of the soul of Hekate). He continues:

> "Himma creates as 'real' the figures of the
> imagination, those beings with whom we
> sleep and walk and talk, the angels and
> daimons who. . .are outside the imagining
> faculty itself. Himma is that mode by
> which the images, which we believe we
> make up, are actually presented to us as
> not of our making, as genuinely created, as
> authentic creatures. . .Without the gift of
> himma we fall into the modern
> psychological illusions. We misunderstand
> the mode of being of these images, the
> figures in our dreams or the persons of our
> imaginings. We believe these figures are
> subjectively real when we mean imaginally
> real: the illusion that we made them up,
> own them, that they are a part of us,

phantasms. Or, we believe these figures are externally real when we mean essentially real – the illusions of parapsychology and hallucinations. We confuse imaginal with subjective and internal, and we mistake essential for external and objective.[157]

And also:

The objective himma is literalized into the objects of its desire. Imagination is thrown outwards, ahead of itself; and the task is less to take back these projections…but more to leap after the projectile reclaiming it as imagination, thereby recognizing. . .that images always be experienced as sensuous independent bod[ies]. One leaps through the projectile by being compelled. Compulsion becomes will through courage.[158]

The courage that desires and sees through desire is that which the heart requires in order to create will. The willing heart. To bring the power of himma in the imagination to the willing heart again evokes the connection between Hekate and Eros, who together create relationship. Watch the arrow.

Shard 2— Hekate Shadowing Eros

This buzzing thought,
This bee that dives through me:
"Revealing shadow creates eros."
What propels this thought?
Another angle: Revealing that hidden part of ourselves,
Some inferior-feeling part of ourselves creates eros.
How is this for me now?
What lies shadowed is the link between myself and a
  larger sense of life: Self. Is that it?
I mean that link between me and an Other, me
And divine nature, me and Hekate.

—Shira Marin

Hekate lurks here but only intuitively, not the ego's
logical connection. I know that Hekate's revealing
herself to me creates eros because I feel the weight
of non-actualized promise wanting to manifest.
She is for me the energy of the arrow that springs
from the bow of Eros. It is Hekate who darts far
and penetrates her mark to the core, through two
hearts, one to the other, a heart-to-heart chat, a
soul connection, Plato's souls, each half finding the
other.

Owen and I talk over this idea that shadow
can create eros. We are in the midst of analyzing it
when I am distracted by Hekate, who is sitting on
the love seat next to the fireplace with a look that
tells me that this pursuit with Owen is headed in
the wrong direction. Suddenly, I pipe up that the
problem in our discussion is that we don't share
the same experiential reality. This is the very point
of Hekate's presence. When Owen asks me for an

example, I tell him that Hekate is sitting behind him under the purple gladioli. He asks about her hair and eye color and dress. When I tell him black, white, and red, he inquires about her shoes. In that her feet are hidden behind a table in front of the chair, I am unable to answer that. Owen: "You should be writing fiction."

I: But this is my reality.

O: Your subjective reality.

I: Yes, to you, subjective, but, to me, objective as in, what comes imaginally from the psyche is equal to what you call the objective truth of philosophy.

O: But evidence would bear out by the thousands that Hekate is not sitting in that seat.

I: True, but that is the problem we face today. We need to expand reality to include a visionary aspect so that what you are calling my fiction can be taken as fact, even if only my private fact, and experienced at least proximally by your parade of thousands. What I call visionary is really a direct experience of the psyche. Certainly Bernadette of Lourdes, the children of Fatima, Teresa of Avila, and Hildegard von Bingen would grasp this sense of reality. In fact, the filmmaking of Alfonso Arau in "Like Water for Chocolate" and Alejandro Inarritu in "Birdman" express this imaginal, psychological expression quite excellently.

Others in the world obviously are at least toying with the idea: Not long ago I noticed a two-day seminar on this sense of life that is being offered at Grace Cathedral.

By the end of our conversations, the strength of Hekate's presence had given me a creative connection to my writing and to Owen that I hadn't had in some time. To my surprise, Owen, in his own way, acknowledged Hekate. There she lived in the shadow of this moment and what came out of it: eros! See! Yes, that is my wish for you. Then, you will know Hekate and her blessing. You will want a deep, loving, open eros with her, I promise.

Hekate shadowing Hera and Zeus

IF HERA AND ZEUS STAND ARCHETYPALLY FOR WOMAN and man brought together by Eros and transformed into wife and husband, Hekate, as she who flies under the arrow, is the force of their transforming and the forging of their link over time.

[Fig. 50]

Ginger Moon for Hekate

Begin with an empty page and a heart unsure,
a famine of thoughts, a fear of no feeling—
just begin from here, from this electricity. [159]

—Natalie Goldberg

MARY HULL WEBSTER, AN ARTIST I KNOW, SUGGESTED
just sitting down before the blank drawing pad
and staring into its space waiting to see what
would emerge. I like this idea; it evokes the
conjurer-woman in her and in me. I love her
certainty when she speaks about this effort as a
possibility for something original to happen:
"[Look and] you will see what needs to appear. . .
a line, a shape, an idea. . .a movement takes place,
a conjunction between your body and the paper. . .
a personal record. . .a unique gesture [of]. . .colors
and shapes, feelings an idea."

Hekate would approve: This effort is no less
than an invocation of Hekate's power. After all,
Hekate is the visionary goddess who whips up wind
from the depths, causing a creative storm.

Astounding art has this potency of something
coming up from that place; it has the energy of the
psyche animating it, and so has Hekate, the goddess
of these creative storms, supporting the arising and
forming of the creative impulse that an artist sends
out into the world. In this way, Hekate surely has
always manifested in life, but only in a very hidden
and subconscious way. Until now!

I noted earlier that the ancient Greeks called Hekate "many-formed"; they grasped her instinctual shape-shifting nature, which was attributed, in later times, to the god Hermes, to shaman, and to all trickster types. Artists have not known her or honored her as the transfiguring goddess that she is. So they don't see her alive in every form of artistic expression. They don't imagine her sacred femininity in their work. What would happen if artists recognized the great value of Hekate as the source of their creative expressions and appealed to her to support them? If you make art, do any creative work whatsoever, consider Hekate; consider her deeply and with love. Considering her as an act of love for yourself. Really!

In consultation with clients, in speaking publicly, with everyone looking for something they can't quite express, the question of profound meaning, the deepest truth, the source of exquisite pain or despair, Hekate is alive. I work gently, wave-like, to bring her into visibility, like tumbled shells and smoothed shards of sea glass onto a salty shore. There, impressed into the sand, into the restive soul, a companionable relationship with Hekate's essence begins to grow deep, burrowing evermore into consciousness the desire and capacity to fully express the truth of being.

Returning to my experience with Mary Webster, using words as my form, I began Mary's exercise by sitting down to page 1, the first of a 30-day writing experiment dedicated to Hekate. Staring into the white, I found the title of the present piece. Finding my dog Ginger's AKC-registered name there surprised me. What is Ginger doing here now? Then I realized: clearly, bright, golden- red Ginger was named by Hekate.

Several months before, I made the final decision to get a female Chow Chow pup, and the word "ginger" popped constantly into my awareness. I chanted it like a mantra without knowing why. One day my friend Pauline called to tell me she had a wonderful young Chow Chow she thought would be just right for me and that I should meet her. When I saw the dog, my heart burst with joy. There she was, golden red like a burnished autumn moon, scorching dark eyes, and an appropriate low, rolling growl of introduction. She skipped backward to stand her ground. I politely extended my hand for a sniff of approval and Pauline said, "Meet Ginger!" Well, what do you think about that? Several months is about 14 weeks and here she was: 14-week-old Ginger. One needn't look far to see Hekate in the background of our meeting. Since Ginger came to live with us at the exact time that I began to write the book, I believe Hekate sent Ginger as her animal familiar to sit under my desk and guard my creative work day and night. And she did for 15 years.

Recall Goethe

PEOPLE TALK ABOUT HEKATE ALL THE TIME WITHOUT knowing it. To wit, Goethe said: "…Whatever you can do, or dream, you can begin it. Boldness has genius, power and magic in it."

I cannot read this comment without considering Hekate. Goethe describes her nature and force exactly. I can feel her vibrate in the words and sense her nearness urging me to create in her honor. Hekate is present, rarely visible at the center but invisibly always a generating force. She is the feminine One who generates, initiates, and propels creative acts. We can evoke Hekate with the words and images we choose and with those that choose us. Mostly we do this unconsciously. What if we did it consciously and intentionally? What would happen if we readily acknowledged the energy of mystery that she brings and wants to have available to us daily—always? What fearless, creative good could arise from such embrace!

Between Heart and Bowels

To write Hekate
no blood: my face
drained to match brows and lashes
now white like the Trinities in December

on walls of face
words sing   become hidden
but look between heart and bowels
there   tiger and raccoon square off
wearing beaglepuss glasses   one man pays
respects
two dogs growl red and black stand guard
over angel with gold milagro heart at
her shoulder left you find
truth is fiction
and fiction true
you find Hekate

—Shira Marin, 1989

[Fig. 51]

A Poet Dreams

A woman dreams:

I'm at my desk, concentrating on something.
I look up, suddenly, there is a face at the
window right in front of me: a large,
wrinkled old woman's face surrounded by
fierce, blonde-gray hair. The face looks so
threatening that I'm terrified. I turn away
and half wake up. I think, "I should greet my
monsters," and I have some feeling that this
woman might be Scandinavian—an
ancestor? I'm not out of the dream, really, as
I think of this, and I find myself going back
to the window. The face is still there, and I
approach it, wanting to be friendly. But she
growls, "Want to make love to you," which
terrifies me even more than the face itself,
and I really do wake up, startled by what
might be awaiting me.

Virtue No Garden

Mother this hag her head a broken river
Some debt I didn't know I had
unholy

mother her skull at my window is all the
animals she has torn
then eaten

and if holy also the wild release
sacred in terror

a debt
my own mother had a Christian name

I intend to comfort horror
my face walks to her
she growls "I want to make love to you"
she is worms
midnight I pray for my own hand
shaking themselves from apples to the grave
were her children goats pigs sacrifice
she asks for union
to kill me to renew herself to renew me to
kill herself

sacred in terror

in the next week there will be hawks there
will be spit to wipe from the floor
there will be a further mother whose feet I
hold
and then a lion
who becomes the one thing I have to do
before I can go on

I cannot say I understand the debt

thunder early autumn
the worms bleed but worms do open soil
she must know love or she wouldn't ask for
it

She is harvest and the danger under harvest
and the everlasting ever-changing ground
beneath the danger
I am stronger this strange year
stronger than what I have known of sheep
of farms of the meadow I thought I would
call dying
I have come a great distance to this window
she is gone now
without my answer
I look to her trees
the winter I will have to learn to carry in
the body that she doesn't have
                              —Holly Prado

HOLLY PRADO'S PIECE IS FILLED WITH EXTRAORDINARY Hekatean images. In a comment to me about her experience of the dream, she said, "I felt, whatever my terror, that it was important to carry something of the hag in myself, not just 'my Christian mother' but the opposite of that. As frightening as this aspect of the goddess can be, I do feel it in me as the old, old woman ancestor who doesn't put up with any [sugar-coated] sweetness, ever, but holds a truth unvarnished."

Though it is possible to look at the words, pick phrases, and perform analysis based on what scholars say about Hekate's nature, the depth of this poem and the nature of Hekate are inside the words themselves. Say them. Breathe them into your body and exhale them as speech. Speaking Hekate gives her body, embodies her in you!

During the Renaissance, Marcilio Ficino said to put soul in the center of our lives. I wonder if he knew that we would, then, put Hekate at the center of our lives. we would, then, put Hekate at the center of our lives. What does the Renaissance have to do with our needs right now? Hekate then: Hekate now when the Feminine Principle of relatedness is everything that can help us.

It is 2016. We are in dire need of saying, "Yes!"

[Fig. 52]

Mother and daughter, Hekate and I

I VISITED GREEN APPLE BOOKS TODAY, ONE OF MY
favorite haunts: very homey and so wonderfully well
stocked. On this trip, I was trying to locate two
psych books and *Between Ourselves*, a collection of
letters written between mothers and daughters. I
couldn't help wondering what it would be like to
have the correspondence between Hekate and me
included in this collection. It seems a suitable place
for such letters between the Deep Mother and
deepening with her daughter.

Then my attention was pulled every which way.
I couldn't help noticing that wherever I turned, I saw
the word "soul." Was I in Christian Limbo?
Purgatory? Surely, I was in a world yearning to
regain soul. And although soul is coming through
other means, there is a tremendous beckoning of
soul through words, as soul translates from the
Greek: *psyche*. But the beckoning isn't only through
words. Following Russell Lockhart's work in *Words
as Eggs*, I want to repeat that soul lives within
words, generally, as the psyche lives in them.

Wonderful! People are noticing we've lost soul,
lost psyche, but few people know we have lost
Hekate, nor do they know her vocabulary. Hekate,
lost in words, is now coming back up from under
words. A start. Probably there are many false starts,
but that is how life unfolds: with false starts, wrong
turns, dead-ends. These are also Hekate's byways.
But many people want to feel this quality of life
again, to be moved by it. Without knowing it, isn't

this another way of saying that we want Hekate back, to feel her and to let her guide a sense of life that we have lost contact with? Yes, you bet it is!

So, *yes,* I am impelled to write Hekate out of our oblivion, to give her words again, felt and heard with inner and outer ears. I am compelled by the state of our world because I so deeply trust that what she brings from her feminine ground of being wants to burst from within us to bring a truly new, if at once ancient, sense of life, always present but long forgotten.

We people actually want to be moved ongoing by soul as Hekate is soul. A favorite word of the day, soul has a number of specific meanings; it is, as you will see, like Hekate, many-formed. Take the *American Heritage Dictionary* definitions for examples:

> *SOUL: The animating and vital principle in [humans] credited with the faculties of thought, action, and emotion and conceived as forming an immaterial entity distinguished from but temporally coexistent with [the human] body.*
>
> *The spiritual nature of human beings, regarded as immortal, separable from the body at death, and susceptible to happiness or misery in a future state;*
>
> *The disembodied spirit of a dead human being; a ghost; a shade;*

*A central or integral part of someone or
thing; the vial core;*

*A person considered as the perfect
embodiment of an intangible quality;*

A person considered as an inspiring force;

*The emotional nature of [humans] as
opposed to [their] intellect or mind;*

*An aggregate of elemental qualities that
enables one to be in harmony with oneself
and to convey to others the honest and
unadorned expression of the hard side of life;*

Derived from [Black people] or their culture.[160]

Is there any definition here that does not somehow
reflect Hekate's particular nature?

Inklings of her Coming at Santa Sabina Center

Dear Hekate,

This afternoon working at my desk, out of the corner of my eye, I can't help my distraction, though batting an eyelash will be enough noise to send them running: two does and their fawns young enough to exhibit white-spotted backs. Irrepressible, the babies spring about in the grass. The mothers eat.Mother and Child Reunion: Hekate, you must be here in this writing. Are you here with me? Sometimes, it seems to take so long for you to make yourself visible. Or is it that, still, I miss you? Sometimes, I am a fawn-child lost in the woods, crying to get close to you. Gazing out the window from my study, I know that there is no feeling in life like that

[Fig. 53]

*one of standing next to you in the shadow
of the great pine. To grow beside you as
your daughter into womanhood and to
reflect your beauty is your precious gift to
me. In showing tenderness, you tell me the
secret of your woman-goddess being. I
learn from you and come into my own.*

Yours,
Shira

I dream:

*I watch myself forming a face over my raw
face and ask what makes me mold many
disguises of myself.*

What are your dreams of "becoming"?

Dear Hekate,

*They call you, "Many-formed." What is that
fact of your nature? Your traits appear in
others—goddesses, gods, animals—in so-
called inanimate objects. Is it your desire to
be expressed this way, indirectly now, when
before you were honored openly, unveiled,
directly? Over time, so much mystery came
to shroud your image, which long ago was
unified and clear. Are these many separate
pieces meant to be stood under to be
understood, taken for your reality? Must our
eyes, our vision with the help of the psyche,
with your very own help, provide the glue
that re-creates your unity? Let me know. I
await your answer.*

Yours,
Shira

[Fig. 54]

Many-formed Hekate:
The Life of Instinct

TO SAY "INSTINCTIVE LIFE" IS TO INVOKE HEKATE: RED, black, purple irises steaming; stones sweating; moss, hares, birds, horses, lions, dogs, frogs.

HEKATE
ANIMALI

[Fig. 55]

*The round golden eye of the animal is like a
seed of light in the darkness, for the creative
powers also possess the possibility of insight
and consciousness. Like the [Hekatean] eye
of a bird, it focuses on the far rather than
the near. The animal is sort of a Behemoth,
the dark female side of God, waiting to be
liberated from its prison on the depths of
the earth.*[161]

—Marie-Louise von Franz

[Fig. 56]

Animali Hekate

*Part of our problem as humans who must
embody spirit in matter is that we don't see
the animal as subtle. We think only of the
spiritual as subtle, rarefied, enlightened. We
dismiss the animal as primitive and gross,
forgetting that sleek slyness of animal
movement and grace of instinct, which guides
the animal at every turn. Empowering [her]
to survive.*[162]

And again:

*The animal heart directly intends, senses, and
responds as a unitary whole. Wholeness in
the act, as a quality of the act.*[163]
—James Hillman

...The animal pads where no one walks.[164]
—Pablo Neruda

[Fig. 57]

Hare-piece: Hekate's Multiplication

. . .like a bunny. Wild hare. Stray hare.
Instinct to create. Not just divide but
multiply. Not just many-formed but lots and
lots of bunnies into rabbits, hares-quick-like!

[Fig. 58]

White Moon Cat: White Moon Cow

THE CAT BASTET WAS SOMETIMES WORSHIPPED AS THE
Egyptian goddess Hathor, who was worshipped as a
cow, the most placid of all animals. In this aspect,
the cat as cow became a great nourisher who
brought and sustained vegetable life not only of the
living but also of the dead.[165] The moon and death
aspects common to both cat and cow bring us into
Hekate's reality. See how she is shown in Greek art,
a tri-form with the head of a cow.

[Fig. 59]

GOD (-DESS) is DOG
Spelled Backward!

WHERE DO GOD AND DOG BEGIN AND END?
Like a bull, the insertion point charges at me: "When
are you going to start writing, and what are you
going to say? "Ginger eyes me insistently and ambles
into the study. She licks my ankle. I tell her, "We're
writing." She nudges me, circles around, and lies
down beside my chair. I look around the room, can't
sense what wants saying, feel somehow like the dogs
when nothing is stimulating their interest. I believe
they pass no judgments on such experiences. Ginger
looks at me expectantly. She watches while I sit there
waiting to be inspired. And the desire for inspiration
is, itself, compelling. At times like these, I have to
cast away the need for inspiration as a basis for
work. I am aiming to work with the ordinary, to just
roost, or graze, or crouch, or lay as necessary. All of
these I can do in my writing. I can vegetate in it like
animals in a barnyard, like Ginger at my feet.

Calling All Animals

Not long ago, I got so desperate to keep steady the spinning plates of my life that I implored the *I Ching*, please, to advise but simply with just one hexagram.[166] Do you know that it did? Thank you, Thank you.

Usually, when I cast the *I Ching*, I dread getting changing lines. They always mean long arduous work at sorting out deep meanings in a sense of time for which I fear I own the wrong clock. When does the actual change occur; how am I to tell? Finally, I can answer this question more often than not.

The more I lean toward my writing with the *I Ching* as a companion, the more accurate I sense I am in developing this naturally psychic sense of time, what the ancients called *kairos*. It is not something abstract. To grasp it one must develop temporal physicality: palpable time. One must feel one's inner ticking and how it beats in unison or counterpoint to that of the universal psyche. This psychic time may or may not be different from my own. When I am following the psyche with the benefit of the Chinese *Word*, it provides a specific frame of reference that I have invited to interact with my inner, subjective reality.

Today, I was casting the *I Ching*, feeling particularly open but focused; then, I noticed my mind stray to the question, "What animal will I be when I write today?" It just popped out of psychic nowhere. The line I cast as I was having this thought turned out to be a changing line. The dreading part of me cursed, but gently. I went on and, again, my mind was distracted by the animal question. Another changing line! These lines were placed in the third and top positions of the hexagram, both masculine turning into feminine lines. The "Taming Power of the Great" changing to "Approach." This was my comment on how to come back into the world of my writing with renewed feeling and confidence that I can make quality and quantity in my life as a writer. Look what happened:

#26 – *Ta Ch'u: The Taming Power of the Great—keeping still, mountain over creative, heaven*

From the Judgment, I learned that I needed to hold firm by holding together, by remaining as focused as possible, to hold back by keeping still, and to remain steadfast as to nourish the holding process.

The idea of "holding" interests me, especially in the sense of holding that is embracing and containing. Great power is needed to hold that which is powerfully great.

I look at the two trigrams, *ken* and *ch'ien*, and get an imaginal sense of the idea of the great holding the great. "Ken" means "Keeping still, mountain," and "ch'ien," "the Creative, Heaven." What image greater on the planet than a mountain to bring creative inspiration down to earth. It should be substantial and firm enough to hold the most powerful heavenly impulse. The commentary on the oracle says that both trigrams point to clarity, truth, and the daily renewal of character. Through such daily renewal one can continue at the height of one's powers, which have been held firmly and so stored up.

Meanwhile, I despair of finding my animal. I think I have rarely, if ever, experienced the *I Ching* as speaking insignificantly or indirectly to me. I couldn't quite figure this turn of the moment. I moved on to read the image and its comment.

Comment on the Image: Heaven within the mountain points to hidden treasure. In the words and deeds of the past lie a hidden treasure that can strengthen character through application of the knowledge of history to give actuality to the past.

The enactment of historical knowledge appeared to be referring to my writing the research I'd found on Hekate. In other words: Get to the keyboard. Find the still place inside, go deeply, find the buried treasure that Hekate is, and record it as my grasp of it dictates.

> *Strength of character and daily renewal*
> *will support you on your journey.*

Good news! Yet, I persisted in my stated wish as impetus for my first step. About the moment I had this thought, I found myself at *9 in the 3rd place*, my first changing line. My thoughts drifted back to the question about the animal I would be in the course of my writing work with Hekate. The line responded:

A good horse that follows others. . .
Awareness of danger,
With perseverance, furthers,
Practice chariot fighting and armed defense
daily.
It furthers one to have somewhere to go

I laughed. A horse, Hekate's mare, will carry me
on this day's journey. My own Pegasus. Immediate
relief in being accompanied by horse power! I was
not completely surprised to find that the comment
here was:

The way opens; the hindrance has been cleared
away. Now, a part of me with strong will could
follow the lead of creative life like one good horse
following another. But, as is often the case, there is a
danger; I needed to use my strength—energy of
desire, courage, and trust in my steps—to remain
aware of my strength, or loss of firmness—faith,
commitment, and direction—can result. That and
protecting oneself against unseen dangers are what
make the practice of keeping one's direction
essential. Then, *9 at the top:*

One attains the way of heaven. Success.

This line speaks for itself. What more could I
need following such an auspicious oracle? But I was
curious and read on.

#19 – Lin/Approach: K'un, the Receptive,
Earth, over Tui, the joyous. Lake.

Distinctly feminine, these images. I hadn't sensed that my lot could become any more pleasing. I hadn't yet considered a particular way with the work. The approach was to be a feminine One. What was this hexagram suggesting?

Lin has many meanings not exhausted by a single word of another language. Its ancient definition from the *I Ching* is "becoming great," which extends to the concept of "approach" as that which is strong and highly placed in relation to that which is lower. A final meaning of the word includes the idea of setting to work on affairs, making efforts, and trusting them.

> *The Judgment: Approach has supreme success. Perseverance furthers. When the eighth month comes, there will be misfortune.*

I notice that often the oracle includes a sense of danger or evil that must be watched for in advance so that it can be dealt with before it becomes reality or so that one can master it. This idea is clearly an aspect in the judgment of this hexagram. Honestly, I probably missed the darkness I needed to be aware of at that time. The work has been demanding by way of keeping me in its whorl. And the whorl is a Hekatean feminine nature so that within the containment of that spiraling movement, I feel somehow safe. Beyond that security, the hexagram on the whole teems with joyful and hopeful progress toward creating a dwelling place for Hekate. As I follow Hekate, I might discover and approach unavoidable misfortune differently, with grace perhaps?

Sometimes, I see my writing here as a kind of oracle for the renewal and evolution of Hekate's instinctual feminine sensibility, her presence, coming into in the culture right now.

In relation to the animal who inhabits the previous hexagram, but is also part of the entire time of the oracle, I needed to remember that the carrier of instinctive creative life, my good horse (Pegasus of another era) is also Hekate's night mare on whom she tears across the pitch sky at the new moon looking for restive souls, lonely wanderers in need of divine guidance. What evil can come from the flight of that kind of instinct? What good can come of it: the guidance of the Hekatean instinctual feminine who embraces all, always? Just look with me. Such knowing and trust of this guidance could well yield very different solutions from those who hark to hegemony and war as the only solutions to conflict.

Perhaps the answer comes in part from the image:

> *The earth above the lake;*
> *The image of approach.*
> *Thus, the superior one is inexhaustible*
> *In [her] will to teach,*
> *And without limits*
> *In [her] tolerance and protection of the*
> *people*

Having changed genders in this passage, the message feels more personal. If there is one aspect of my life that feels evil, it's a nagging fatigue that overcomes me when I least expect it or wish it from driving so hard, just as this society has taught me. For all the astounding energy I've experienced over these years of tracking Hekate, of being dogged by her, nothing feels more limiting of my desire than this one thing. Yes, I've always been able to endure and will continue in this work. And perhaps the message is to live in such a fashion that my will and desire to do this work for Hekate, though modest, continues, and that I will be tolerant of those who oppose it and find it a challenge. I will protect those who are wandering unwittingly, waiting for her to guide them through the gate of their own psyches, each in his or her own time. I will foster them as Hekate does, learn to foster myself as she would have me do as an expression of her intention to indwell, to act steadily, just steadily. Steady as she goes.

Come along; travel through; cross the threshold into the landscape of your own psyche. Carl Jung did and, clearly, he created much good in the world. We can, too!

[Fig. 60]

Hekate and Dog: Kereberus the 3-headed Hell-hound

"*Cerberus, associated by the Dorians with the dog-headed Egyptian god Anubis who conducted souls to the Underworld, seems to have originally been the Death-goddess Hekate. . . she was portrayed as a bitch because dogs eat corpse flesh and howl at the moon.*"[167]

—Robert Graves

[Fig. 61]

Chaldean Hekate's Daemon-dogs

*. . .For indeed from the womb
of the earth rush forth earthly dogs that never
reveal a true sign to man,*

*Chariotress of the aery, earthly, and
 watery dogs.*[168]

Hekate Thanatoio

*To the Greeks, Thanatos, death, is not a
personification but a cloud, a veil, a mist
drifting around the head. The cloud appears
in two colors, black and porphyry (purple). . .
[The veil of Thanatos] is a physical veil, a
cloud between man and light, a private
fragment of night for creatures of the day.*[169]

Ker is the agent of Thanatos, perhaps more personal
and dangerous. "The *ker* of Thanatos can knock a
man down and master him; no one can duck and

[Fig. 62]

avoid her, she is ten thousand." On the battlefield,
"she has hands and drags corpses by the heels; she
has jaws and will later have claws. She is the poetic
equivalent of. . .

> *the corpse-ravagers of*
> *war the birds and dogs,*
> *or the sphinxes*
> *Sirens and*
> *Harpies ghosts. . .*
> *lust*
> *disease*
> *moral lack*
> *sister of sleep, death and the furies.*
>
> *She is winged,*
> *attractive and*
> *repulsive.*[170]

Following his death, the Greek Patroklos declared:

> *The frightening ker who got me by lot when I*
> *was born has opened her jaws around me. . .*
> *She is analogous to kind black earth opening*
> *to swallow men, like an animal swallowing*
> *her young, like Kereberos the biter, or the*
> *terrible stomion, the mouth to the underworld*
> *. . .in Plato's hell which roars when any*
> *unpurified soul tries to escape.*[171]

[Fig. 63]

Ker Thanatoio

KER THANATOIO IS THE AGENT OF DEATH. SHE IS "NOT
death-goddess of death, *but of darkness*. Without
Ker, Thanatos is less personal and less fatal. . .

> *The Greeks had no word for irreversible
> death. One does not die; one darkens. There
> is then always the hope of the little interior
> light of intelligence, which may never go
> completely out inside the psyche, but waits to
> be aroused by a human gesture like the
> oldest form of Sleeping Beauty. The psyche is
> memory and intelligence dormant, and can
> under proper circumstances, be recalled by
> grief, love, magic, or poetry.*[172]

Hekate's name is never mentioned in this text,
but is there any denying that she constellates here?
But this is the point of phenomenology, of what Russ
Lockhart calls *cultivating* or circling, as one does
with a dream or other spontaneous images arising
from the psyche: Images can then constellate without
having to correspond exactly.[173] Hekate alive in them,
imbues them with new life and meaning, reveals
itself from within the image instead of having
meaning assigned to it from an outer source.

In a footnote, I note that the most interesting
part of my search for the etymology of *ker and
keres* was discovering the associations to Hekate,
Hades, and the gods who clean the corpses from
the battlefields. Its etymology, though unsub-
stantiated, may be related to the Semitic word for
"cherub."[174] A reference to winged Hekate? *Hekate
Angelos?* Maybe.

[Fig. 64]

Hekate as Dog:
Shadow at the Threshold

I dream a fragment:

Then, commotion. I go into the living room and am shocked to see that the room doesn't look like mine. The rugs on the floors are verdigris "throws" of cheap shag. I can't believe my eyes, look closer, and see that three or four German Shepherd dogs are lying in wait; two are frisking in and out of the front door. There are big piles of dung on the floor. My colleague discovers this scene with me. His reaction is quiet but concerned. I'm not mad at the dogs, but the mess is painful. I begin to clean it up before we leave.

And another:

I dream:

It is morning. My dog Ginger comes to the side of my bed, looks at me squarely, and lets go a tremendous gush of urine on the floor. I woke with a jolt.

Musing on the dream: The place I live is no longer where I know.

Ginger Loves Me, This I Know . . .

I KNOW THAT I AM NOT THE ONLY ONE WHO UNDERSTANDS that this work comes from some seemingly inarticulable place within me. Even since the beginning of this writing, others have an ear tuned to that place beyond where the human ego can go. It's an Other world, the psychological world from which Hekate speaks. Generally, I don't know what I'm going to write until I sit down, although sometimes I feel hounded in inexplicable ways, like being followed by a dog who knows I have a treat in my pocket.

Trust. I'm stuck with the demand to trust that the psyche, the Other world, will articulate itself through Hekate onto the page and give these words their natural depth. Ginger appears again. What a companion and guardian she is at the door of my study; she sits like Hekate, steadfast keeper of the gate. She is the key to opening, to crossing over into the psyche's landscape, to her world, her vitality, her truth, the truth she wants to share with all of us. We are discovering this truth together—you and I—on this journey. Ginger grasps the moment; she knows the inarticulable place. She is it. Ginger carries the instinct to eros; the utter connectedness between us astounds me.

The obvious question: How has the depth from which I need to speak about Hekate related to Ginger and me? What does she know of words; she'll sit by me whether I'm writing or not. She responds to that heart place that senses, feels, knows truth without words. This is her truth. It is Hekate's truth expressed through Ginger, her animal familiar. Is that the message that Ginger brings from the psyche this morning?

Hekate is the undeniable, forceful truth of instinctual life; she is strong like Ginger when she is charging over the hill and through the grass. Hekate truly is the authority on which this work rests. Hekate is who Natalie Goldberg calls "wild mind," who Mary Oliver evokes when she describes a "wild and precious life," what Federico Garcia Lorca calls *duende*. Hekate inhabits that meeting point begtween what is above and what is below, that fulcrum of the union of opposites in Jung's sense of the archetypal Self. This is the truth that is Hekate. Hekate's truth is the blood that must course through this body of language, give words to this life, and restore our full vision of her as both the still and the wild heart of language.

Artist and writer friends, Fran and Jane, and I were talking recently about expressing Hekate's realm into the outer world. What language is right for that expression? Always the question is not only of what I want to say, but what wants to be said by Hekate so that she lives wholly in the material world and in us, resurrected in the conscious psyche.

That is Hekate's goal: to indwell, to come alive again, to re-animate within us fully and to be reflected out into the world. She wishes to be seen as we do and to have her reality reflected back so that she knows she exists, just as she wishes this for us. She has come in so many forms and is now more fully expressed through this writing. It's taken so much imagery and so many words to convey her nature and to see the value of awakening her, reawakening the mystery we yearn to live. Doing so is the other pole of what Thoreau noted when, as a man of his time, "The mass of men lead lives of quiet desperation."[175] The choice, it appears, is to follow the path Thoreau describes or to spend our lives reassembling the shards of Hekate's broken mystery. Hers is a life-affirming adventure filled with all manner of teeming life. Each of us has to decide!

Through all of this writing, my goal has been to express Hekate's shards of being in a language suitable for Hekate's telling. I have been aware of needing what Russ Lockhart calls "alchemical language," layers of speech that combine dark and light with the paradoxical intention that is at the core of Hekate's nature: the sacred expressing itself, sometimes in profane terms. Our human experience can bring together what is above and what is below by using speech that seeks to grasp the two at once, that perceives and experiences the one in the other. In this context, the alchemical saying, "As above, so below," takes its place. The need to remain intimate with this aspect of telling Hekate's story weighs on me. It is the imperative of speaking the truth of the psyche that belongs to Hekate. But we must realize that Hekate's truth and ours is not only clay and earth, but the outer reaches of space and the depths of the Underworld.

Hekate's truth is found even in the underworld of academia which, otherwise, is a world of almost solely rationalistic thinking. Hekate claims in an ancient oracle:

"I dwell behind the Father's thoughts, I, the Soul, who with heat, do ensoul all things."[176]

Hekate can be easily found in scholarly works of a phenomenological or descriptive nature. In fact, researching and living with Hekate sometimes has involved a sacrifice of rationalistic intellect. To begin to know Hekate necessitates seeing without understanding, what phenomenology calls "apprehending" with the eyes, the ears, the tongue, and the nose of imagination. This act invokes the unconscious psyche to show what has not before been visible: images as instinct, as James Hillman said, that we can come to *experience* as knowledge. Experience *as* knowledge.

Elsewhere I noted that the language of Hekate is untamed, a dog barking, sniffing the ground to find its buried treasure and drag it into the upper world. So, Ginger, as Hekate's familiar, with her nose for the *numinous*, for the sacred, bridges the two worlds for me. The level of instinct that she encourages in me animates another dimension of my desire to write. Yes, desire, replacing discipline, has become the imperative for my work. I love you, Ginger!

A woman dreams:

I call Shira to ask if I can come to her house. I go to her house, but she is in bed. A fawn-colored German Shepherd answers the door and lets me in.

Hekate Canidae

ELEANORA WOLOY SAYS THAT OUR *NEED* TO "RELATE
to the non-human environment and the ability to
include others in our social responses. . . was the key
to the bond [between humans and dogs]." I can
imagine that Hekate with her companion dogs is the
archetypal image behind Woloy's comment in that
she believes her idea to be the basis of the
domestication of dogs.[177] By the way, more than
30,000 years have passed since dogs joined the
human family. It is little wonder that we often have
stronger bonds with them than we do with our
spouses!

Imagine that Hekate has given dogs an extraordinary role through time. What Great Goddess
other than Hekate would have called male votaries
Kelobim, meaning "dogs"? Dogs were not anthrop-
omorphized; men were theriomorphized! Remember:
Cerberus, who guards the gates of Hell, is a three-
headed dog, often identical with Hekate herself. As
Hekate presides over the threshold, so does the dog.
Do you wonder why so often your own animal sits
by the front door protecting all life within from the
life without?

Our psychic relation to animals and specifically
to dogs is well documented. Our relationship plays
out in the cycle of life—birth, death, and rebirth.
Grieving relatives buried dogs with the dead as
psychopomps, guides in the underworld, and were
part of ritual death sacrifice for the purpose of
purification. Stories of dog sacrifices held at the

crossroads and dogs standing guard between the worlds of the living and the dead are common in Greek mythology. The same is true of a number of Native American tribes: the Iroquois, the Huron, the Seminole, the central Eskimo, and some Ojibwa. I note these to suggest the widespread feeling for the *dog as a change agent*, as one who, together with Hekate in human form, "transmutes instinct into spirit, thus bringing rebirth." Even in alchemical texts the dog is considered "an apt synonym for the transforming substance."[178] So, even as this creature watches over death's doorstep, because it belongs to the paradoxical nature that is Hekate's, it contains the seed of rebirth.

There was a time when wolf and dog were called by the same name. Over so much time, we have interacted with dogs in so many ways that speak of their relation to Hekate. Equally Hekatean but less well known is the fact that dogs were the helpers of the Shaman and the embodiment of the prophetic gift of the Shaman. According to a Siberian Shaman, spirits of the cave were invisible to all except a few gifted [shaman] and dogs.[179]

Are you wondering what makes the dog Hekate's most special familiar and companion? Above all other animals, we have been given the dog as our most faithful animal companion. Even if we do not love dogs best or at all consciously, even if one is afraid of them, dogs are as true to us as the fact that *Hekate's great motherly warmth is with us even when we are completely unaware of her.*

Jung remarked that *instincts are the vital foundations that govern all life.*[180] My unleashed fantasy is that within the dark recesses of Jung's mind he included Hekate, the goddess, with her dog. Barbara Hannah, a Swiss Jungian analyst and direct student of Jung's, described dog instinct as that which one does that is just right, that one knows absolutely in the immediate moment. This is the presence of not just any energy but primordial instinctive life driven by Hekate's theriomorphic image, our archetypal dog nature. From the underworld, on the haunches of her adamantine clarity, Hekate's dog nature drives us toward the requirements of the moment.[181]

In 1991, a local radio station broadcast news of a study that supported a notion instinctively known to be true: that many people value their dogs almost as much as (if not equally or more than) they value other family members. You can imagine the level of attachment in these households, considering that the dog provides essential unconditional love! The need for attachment is a biological instinct rooted in nurturance, care-giving, and emotional and physical closeness that life with a dog friend offers us: a gift from Hekate. What is the message for us? In giving us the dog, Hekate gives us a special opportunity for relationship whether we enjoyed it early in life with our parents or not.

The Great Dog Mother
Loves the Challenged

IN MY OWN BACKYARD, AN AMAZING VIETNAM VET IN A
hooded red sweatshirt wheels like the wind in his
chair down and up the hills of our neighborhood.
Without legs, but with the arms and shoulders of
Atlas, through sun or storm, I have seen him make
his way. Nothing stops him. How he touches and
heats the heart of courage in me. Does he have a dog
at home?

Hekate loves wheelchair residents, whose way
lies at the end of red-tipped canes, and those for
whom the world is all but silent—anyone disabled.
She has sent her most loving and able creature up
from the depths and down from the heavens, *her*
own best companion, to support the efforts of these
souls in their daily routines to heal their ostensibly
broken lives. Hekate loves the specially challenged,
those who face the world with pieces missing from
their most intimate experience, their bodies. But
then, as the goddess of primordial instinct, pieces,
dismemberment, and restoration, Hekate can send
the healing power of her favorite animal to help, to
fill in a vital missing part.

Walking in Marin County one summer day, I
noticed a man sitting in some grass so that only his
rib cage up was visible. He looked as if he just grew
out of the ground. "Truly birthed out of Mother
Earth," I thought. Nearing the place where he sat, I
realized it wasn't so at all. This extraordinary man
had survived a horrifying accident that had claimed
his body from the chest down, yet he had committed

to making as fulfilling a life as he could in his extraordinary circumstances. What miracle of life was this: someone grounded profoundly in the archetype of Mystery.

Dogs are special helpful creatures that might have descended from the dog Hekate bestowed upon Asclepius. Legend has it that Asclepius always had his dog beside him as a companion and healing assistant. The Greek physician Asclepius, the hero-god with chthonic and celestial attributes akin to Hekate's, must have been her emissary as healer. Along with the dog, Asclepius used Hekate's language, the language of images, the dream, to heal those who came to his temple.[182] With a dog as complement, the challenged can function more wholly. A life that may have felt dead is reborn through the care of a dog. What, if not this, connects the challenged most deeply with Hekate.

The new sense of the disabled as challenged must come from Hekate's realm because she embodies the paradox of wounding and healing and most definitely stands for that Chinese character that depicts the simultaneous conditions of crisis and opportunity. Oh, what the Chinese have known for centuries!

Finally, we are conceiving what the specially challenged have to offer. To wit, the extraordinarily inspiring prose of Christopher Nolan is a truly great gift. Writer Nancy Mairs and actress Marlee Matlin have given much to us from their worlds. And of a world much farther away, cosmologist and theoretical physicist Stephan Hawking comes immediately to mind. Consider Beethoven, who composed music though he was becoming deaf, and Michelangelo, sculpting though increasingly blind. Remember when we used to call these people "handicapped"?

Benevolent Bitch Mother

IN ANCIENT TIMES, THE GREAT GODDESS HERSELF WAS referred to as a wolf. There was a time when the wolf and the dog were called by the same name and a time when everyone knew both belonged to the She-Wolf of Rome, the Great Mother Goddess Hekate.[183]

Many lupine foster mothers exist in mythology, but most touching to me is the story of Asclepius, the great physician who was suckled by a wolf after being abandoned by his human mother. Dreams became the healing wolf milk for those who came to Asclepius' temple seeking cures for their ills. Consider Hekate, deliverer of dreams, of milk, nursing us with the dream milk of the psyche, the most nourishing, if only we listen. Listen. . . Drink!

Tlingit song

It would be very nice to die with a wolf woman.
It would be very pleasant.

[Fig. 65]

Shard 9: Hekatean Funny or Hekate Goes to the Office

SHE WAS JUST ABOUT TO LEAVE BUT STOPPED SHORT: "Do you have any children?" I wondered what prompted the question, yet said, "I've raised some but haven't been blessed with any of my own. What makes you ask? "Well," she said, "if you do have kids, I bet they'll be just as cute as your dog!"

[Fig. 66]

Shard 10: Hekatean Pith

What Hekate said to K—

A woman teaches her instinct doggedly: "Don't be
a dumb dog chasing after a stick instead of
a juicy bone!"

[Fig. 67]

Furry Moon with Wolf

I dream:

*I woke up singing, singing "Bad Moon
Rising." I see a
Ba-a-a-d Moon Rising.*

From my L.A. poet friend, Holly Prado Northup:

*Your gift of the wolf amazes me: No one has
ever responded to an inner image of mine
with such visual caring and perception. The
wolf; the furred and golden moon; the setting
of white paper as snow, or the landscape of
the psyche on which anything might be
written. . . I'll howl and howl all summer.*

From me:

*I had something else in mind when I made
that furry moon. I had no idea that it was
going to take on that kind of animal nature.
I wasn't even sure I liked it. Following that
through, I began a series of depictions of
psychic revelations. What happened to the
moon surely was ordained by the
unconscious: a howling lunar instinct.
Hekate! We are sisters of the wolf-moon!*

LOBA – Part 1

O lost moon sisters
crescent in hair, sea under foot do you
wander
in blue veil, in green leaf, in tattered shawl do
you wander with
gold leaf skin, with flaming hair do you
wander. . .

. . .under the waning moon, hair streaming in
black rain
wailing with stray dogs, hissing in doorways
shadows you are, that fall on the crossroads,
highways. . .

. . .spitting do you wander
mumbling and crying do you wander
aged and talking to yourselves
with roving eyes do you wander
hot

for quick love do you wander
weeping your dead

naked you walk
swathed in long robes you walk
swaddled in death shroud you walk
backwards you walk

> *hungry*
> *hungry*
> *hungry*

shrieking I hear you
singing I hear you
cursing I hear you
praying I hear you...

> *. . .walk the long night seeking you*
> *I climb the sea crest seeking you*
> *I lie on the prairie, batter at stone gates*
> *calling you names. . .*

. . .I move within you, light the evening fire
I dip my hand in you and eat your flesh
you are my mirror image and my sister you
disappear like smoke on misty hills
gypsy mother, I lean my head on your back

I am you
and I must become you
I have been you
I am always you
I must become you

> *ay-a*
> *ay-aah*
> *ay-a*
> *ah-aahah*
> *maya ma maya ma*
> *om star mother ma om*
> *mayamaah*

. . .If you do not come apart like bread
in her hands, she falls
like steel on your head. The flesh

knows better than the spirit what the soul
has eyes for. Has she sunk
root in your watering place, does she look
with her wolf's eyes out of your head? . . .

From Sketches of the Loba

> . . .*wolf cry you hear*

falls

> *from the stars*
> *the Loba*

dances, she

> *treads the*

salty earth, she

> *dies not*

> *raise*

breath cloud heavenward

> *her breath*

itself

> *is carnage.*[184]

—Diane di Prima

Remember Bastet with Hekate Eileitheia

*Along with other epithets, Bastet was a
goddess of the birth-
    chamber. And like Mother Hekate, along
with other epithets, Bastet
was a mother.*[185]

I dream:

*I see a card covered with all sorts of cats.
They're screeching meowing, yowling. The
caption reads:
Happy Mother's Day!*

[Fig. 68]

Bastet the Vulture?

*Bastet the cat goddess, in her mother aspect,
was a vulture, a virgin vulture who,
while considered strictly underworldly, was
also thought to be
parthenogenic.*[186]

I dream:

*I am supposed to go to a meeting and bring
an animal with me. I go out onto the terrace
of the old stone house I am visiting and see a
number of large wild cats and other animals.
There are lionesses, others I can't name, and
a large black panther picking apart a brown,
black, and white speckled bird. At first, I
don't see that the cat has killed it. I look
closer and see blood, and notice that the cat
has in its mouth the guts of the bird; I'm very
struck by this. I think nature is taking its
course and I let go of my sadness. I get the
sense that the panther is the animal I am to
take with me. Somehow, the others, though
not eating anything, are dangerous. I do have
a sense of what the panther is about; the
others seem less predictable.*

[Fig. 69]

SnakeINcat

...Though the cat is a warm-blooded animal, it has some of the coldness of the serpent. Both are witches' animals and both are used in magic, but that is a stigma which they share with a great many other small animals such as hares, birds. . .[other of Hekate's animals].[187]

Many mythologies tell of a cosmic serpent which lies encircling the whole world, holding its tail in its mouth. . .all-powerful. . .self-begetting. . .[having] no beginning or end. . .Sometimes this image of the coiled serpent merges with the image of the coiled cat.[188]

Are these aspects of Hekate merging? Hekate emerging, encircling the world....

[Fig. 70]

Oh, Mummy!

I dream:

*Red; her blood flows naturally, she comes to
life, transformed. I'm in a kitchen-dining-
living room combination (complex). I am
holding a large glass of water with Spatz, our
female cat, lodged in it. Her head sticks out
of the top so that she looks like a mummy. I
realize that she has to get out of the glass. As
I'm trying to figure out how to do this, the
glass slips from my hand and her head slips
under the water and gets stuck. If I don't
hurry, she'll drown. I throw the glass hard
onto the floor and break it. Spatz lies there.
I'm scared but start pumping her body. She
chokes and spurts water. She's turned ginger
red, stripe-ish, and looks very upset, but I
believe she'll be all right.*

*It is not too far a reach to see this dream as
being related to my consideration of Hekate
driven into darkness, into the Underworld,
and also the necessity of retrieving her. When
she is free, the cat turns red; her blood flows
naturally, she comes to life transformed.
When we massage the truth out of her we
will be enlivened again; our world will be
renewed and transformed.*

*P.S. Later, I came across this picture of Bastet
as a mummy in the Underworld.*

[Fig. 71]

Hekate's God-daughter: Cinders-Cat

SOOTY, MY CAT, BLACK WITH BRASSY BRINDLE MARKINGS, bears an uncanny resemblance to Bastet. That makes her both a child and a familiar of Hekate. Sooty got her name from the fact that she looked, as a kitten, as if she had been born in a pile of ashes that she couldn't shake out of her fur. Nothing could have convinced me then that underneath it all her name connected her with Cinderella the fairy tale, to which I am most drawn. Yes, truly!

The oldest version of Cinderella is Italian, and in the story, the despised and disregarded stepdaughter who lives on the kitchen hearth like a cat and is actually called "Cinders-Cat,"[189] There is also an Irish telling of the tale in which the fairy godmother is a cat. Who more than Hekate is the archetypal Godmother?

Patricia Dale-Green's words stole my breath when I read the following:

> *When the virgin cat-goddess is darkened by smoke and ashes she reminds me of those black Madonnas that are to be seen in French and Italian churches.*[190]

Remember what I said earlier about black Madonnas, the Virgin Mary, and Hekate? Now the Madonna of the Cat enters the scene. In medieval art it is actually common to see the cat in portraits of the Holy Family. And then there is Cinders-cat herself!

Only much later in the French Perriault version called "Cendrillon" did the hearth cat become the young, virginal Cinderella of independent nature, self-possessed, and not unlike the cat!

From long ago, in French politics, the cat symbolized the desire to be liberated from oppression, which is quite a connection back to Cinderella's nodal moments with her god-mother-Hekate, wherein Hekate bestows blessings that allow Cinderella to experience herself and her life in a joyful way. These blessings bestow also on the prince guiding his desire to free himself from oppressive obligation to marry the "correct" wife; he is then free to commit to a woman he can love and who will love him for himself. The prince's discovery of Cinderella's identity frees him to love authentically, and Cinderella is released finally from the oppression of her stepmother's and stepsisters' underdeveloped and masculinized femininity. Like a cat, Hekate, even as godmother, slips in and out of the doors of the psyche, leading instinctively, knowing the way.

[Fig. 72]

"I Reached for Catty."

AFTER SO MANY YEARS, I SEE A LITTLE GIRL PETRIFIED AS she faces the world because. . .Just because! I have learned: Early parental-deaths-paternal-maternal-physical-or-emotional leave a young girl feeling alone. My father died; I was 10. Frozen in some remote land, I could not find embrace. As an adult, I stayed too long, sometimes much too long, with people in psychological spaces, in emotional graveyards, because I literally did not know what I would do to survive. I died at the scene. When something that was bad for me would happen, I would look strong, appear to take it in stride, transcend it, because that is how adults act. I am an actor. The truth: Suddenly, I was 10 years old again, waiting for someone to take care of me. Waiting for someone to come.

Suddenly, memory darts way back. I'm an infant on my back, pushing arms with curled fingers upwards, grabbing the air, trying to bring it closer. Make me warm, keep me warm, and don't leave me. Don't leave me. Not alone. No more, no more. Don't want to be alone no more. I want my mommy, I want my mommy. I WANT MY MOMMY. IWANTMYMOOMMY. III-WAAAANTTT-MMYY-MAHHMMY. No mommy, no mommy, no mommy, no one, no warm. No. Frozen. Afraid. No mommy war, no-afraid mommy. No-saving mommy. Baby me alone afraid, so afraid, too afraid, cold. So cold alone. No-safe-warm-mommy. I stay and reach, nowhere to go. Little skin burns with cold. Freezing feet and knees that kick and beg the air to come warm and close. Tummy heaving, tears and lips wailing for warm mommy. She doesn't come.

I reach for catty.

I reach for Hekate. He-cat-e?

Marie-Louise von Franz commented on the cat as a healing image for the existential fear a woman can suffer because she did not get enough maternal love (*any* good mother figure).[191]

Synchronous, I think, that the woman who had this experience at mid-life and spontaneously reached for a stuffed animal of a rare white tiger which she had bought for her own child. She clutched it to her chest and stoked its fur. She told it she would never ever leave it again. More important: It would never ever leave her.

Hekate does not abandon us. Ever.

The Other Black Cat

NOT THE DESTRUCTIVE ONE. THE SIDE OF HEKATE THAT
most don't know. There is a black cat who heals or
brings clairvoyance. I mean the black cat who
embodies creative un-knowing, who embodies
Hekate and Eros faithfully waiting for the dawn
of the unexpected: the not-knowing that follows the
un-knowing.[192]

A Woman Sends Her Lion Dream

I dream of a lion who wants to mate with me; his name is Rene (reborn). I am afraid of him and of making love with an animal. The lion himself, when I have the nerve to talk to him, tells me that he has plenty of time, not to hurry. He'll wait. I can't believe that any man will wait for me, but I trust that this animal soul—a powerful, fierce image of male self-esteem so lacking, I'm beginning to think—"This father will wait, does care, won't desert me."

From me:
Regarding your lion-mate, rebirth in mating with the powerful leonine instinct, the one

[Fig. 73]

who will truly unite with you no matter your different-ness is really appealing. For me it evokes a primordial aspect of femininity in both women and men that cannot be reached any other way. Hekate wants us to know this part of our nature and so has lions seated at our right and left hands. I meant to say her right and left hands. So, maybe the point is that we need to reach out creatively into the world with this animal sense of making life that's still protected by the instinctual part, that esteems itself, knowing when to mate and when to wait.

THERE IS A STORMING DEBATE AMONG CLASSICISTS AS TO whether lions are connected with Hekate, even though we see them seated beside her in sculptural renderings. Mostly we think of lions in those times as belonging to Apollo, but the truth is that those lions don't represent the searing intellect of Apollo. They have to do with the other side of his nature: his animal, mating nature. In any case, as the lions guard the way of Apollo, you can think of Hekate guarding him. Hekate and Apollo are both guardians of roadways, walled places, openings.

P.S. To my friend: I'm pleased, but not surprised, to hear about this connection with your father-work. I see again and again how we women get into deep difficulty when dad doesn't engender in us the foundation of femininity that comes through positive fatherly admiration of us daughters. Hint, hint, dads!

Two Cats Crouching

PI AND SOOTY HAVE BEEN LIVING UNDER THE BED SINCE my Chow Chow, Ginger, arrived last March 11: Pi-cat's birthday, actually. He should have had birthday cake. The cake tradition, by the way, began with Hekate. Instead, something also like Hekate, Pi, and Sooty-cat ended up in hiding under the bed, in the closets, everywhere but free to roam as they used to before Ginger Moon, our other Hekatean familiar took up residence with us. Feral feline exiled—Hekate exiled.

Chagrined from the beginning of this phase of life in our household, I have worried, fretted, and tried to do anything I could do on my own for these seemingly lost friends. Nothing seems to satisfy in them a sense of safety. Oddly enough, Ginger has always both chased the cats to be near them and play with them and also stayed a truly respectable distance away from them. Unfortunately for all of us, the cats don't grasp what's going on; they don't realize what power they have if only they would seize it. Others said to leave them alone; they'd "get it together." They said, "Give them time to work it out." I have stopped worrying so much; I have set the cats' concerns aside. I set aside anything to do with these creatures who have always been with me in darker times. I observe to see if they will find their instinctive balance.

Suddenly one day, guilt and anger finally rushed to my face. This situation had to change; I could no longer brush off Sooty and Pi, pretending they didn't exist. Attempts to contact animal trainers and even animal psychics had not yielded success. But day by day, I become more inwardly insistent on having those extraordinary felines back in my life. I missed Pi's seemingly vapid stare and finely cut silver-and-black-striped, uptown carriage. And Sooty's eyes that make me tell the truth no matter what! I sit in the bedroom now more often just so I can be with them. At night, the cats know when the dogs have been bedded down in their wire crates. Immediately they come out to sleep with us, burrowing into the covers between Owen and me. Their one joy is with us; mine, too, with them. It is our only grace.

Driven Under

I KNOW THIS LIFE OF BEING "DRIVEN UNDER" ISN'T right or good for them. It reminds me of what happened to Hekate. Sneaking around, dodging dogs: Hekate dodging herself in another aspect. What is encouraging this opposition: the enactment of the myth of fighting cats and dogs?

Sooty and Pi have animal rights. Shouldn't they be exercising them instinctively in relation to the dog? What keeps Hekate from mediating the dispute of these animals descended from the same original creature, the meerkat? What is the psychological

[Fig. 74]

value of this conflict? My dream of a household full of animals certainly hasn't come to pass. So, I give up my dream to wait for new information, but when I consider the cats crouching around the comers of the bed, my fur flies.

This problem under my roof: I can't push away the thought of the larger arena of all animals, animal nature itself, deprived of a proper place in life. Little wonder that certain groups of people make rabid attempts to restore the dignity of animal life. That's Hekate at work.

Touching: This cause is so ardently supported by women. My sister-in-law works vigorously in the field of animal rights; she and I have been talking about the connection between the repression of animal life and that of feminine life in this country. That connection has got to surface in the life of instinct.

Then I dream:

The cats and the dogs see each other across a great chasm. Suddenly, they are on the same side, getting along together splendidly. I think to myself, "Ah, finally!"

[Fig. 75]

For the Birds

Hope is the thing with feathers
That perches in the soul,
And sings the tune without the words,
And never stops at all.[193]

—Emily Dickinson

IMAGINE A 9-YEAR-OLD GIRL WITH A SKY-BLUE PARAKEET. No sooner named than it fell on its back: Dead. I watched more in astonishment than horror. I had revived many a goldfish already in my short years. Something about this son of death was more definite. I was more devastated than I could have imagined. I decided there was more hope in goldfish than in birds. My young ego invested in goldfish. Birds were beyond me; I thought *no more birds.*

But birds keep peeping and pecking their way into my heart, invited or not. In true Hekatean style. Poe's raven and Coleridge's albatross clutched the choice perches in my soul. I remember only one time when I yearned for the Bluebird of Happiness and sang a school song I'd been taught with the same title.

At 23, I longed for birds again, wanted to fly, wondered how that would ever be possible. I got the idea that the matter of flight was creative. What was winged inside me? I despaired of expressing this bird until I realized what the bird whispered in my ear: Hope! The opposite of despair. Not just any hope but hope for a flight of imagination, a lifelong creative expression. I would need to see the

proverbial glass half-full so that my bird would have
something to drink.

Since the days when my tiny pink ballet slippers
pirouetted atop the notes of Swan Lake, I hoped to
glide through life with the creative grace and beauty
of a swan. It was only later that I became aware of
the ugly duckling from which the swan had emerged.
Coming to terms with that duckling, the shadow of
the swan, left me limp with the desire to become a
creature who was assured of becoming more
aesthetically pleasing. Eventually, the image of the
transformation became the driving force of my life
story with such symbolic value that its energy
infused me with indefatigable hope. Emily
Dickinson's hope.

I dream:

Something draws me to look under our bed.
I notice that the rug is shredded, but I'm
aware that the cats no longer live there.
However, covering the expanse is a
patchwork of sod squares with some grass
growing out of them. Under my half of the
bed where 4 squares join, a mallard- green
fledgling pops up and starts looking around.
Then I notice that eggs are everywhere,
tucked under a layer of sod. I feel amazed
and delighted.

Would identifying with birds give me wings?
For many years since, my husband Owen, knowing
nothing of the above, nicknamed me "Birdy." Has

that put me any closer to the Holy Winged, to the inspiration of the Paraclete that, like Love, is not only a momentary blessing but can last a lifetime? The lifelong perch that holds the bird, creative inspiration, the Paraclete, and Love combine to form a bond with sacred life. Over my years, winged Life had beckoned me to fly free whatever that might look like.

And here Hekate insinuates herself; it appears that she has determined most of my life's unfolding. Is it readily visible how the bird brought me closer to the divine Hekate, a goddess having significant bird ancestry? Do you sense her? There is a creative winged-ness in all our lives. Do sense it, will you? It is the creative, self-transforming energy in us that brings us to natural oneness with ourselves.

A further note on Hekate's direct relationship with birds: The way of Greek mythology is to unfold various accounts that explain the genealogies of gods and goddesses. Having 6 accounts herself, Hekate is no exception. Each of these parents allegedly bore Hekate:

Aster and Perses (from Hesiod)
Phoebe and Kiosk (Hesiod)
Sprung from Nyx-Night (from Robert Graves)
Tethys and Okeanos (another daughter is Aphrodite from Robert Graves)
Admetus and Pheaean woman (from Thessalian legend)
Asteria and Zeus (From Musaeus)

Zeus is Hekate's father, and she is his favorite daughter! For genealogical purposes, let's consider Zeus, who briefly became a *swan*. Zeus, swan-lover of Leda, fathered Helen and Phoebe. She bore, in turn, Leto (mother of Artemis and Apollo) and Asteria. Later, Zeus fell in love with but was rejected by Leto's sister, the star Titaness Asteria, mother of Hekate. As Fate had it, according to myth, Leda, the mother of Phoebe, was grandmother to Asteria and great-grandmother of Hekate. Asteria eventually turned herself into a quail and leapt into (or was thrown into) the sea and became the isle Ortygia— Quail Island. Though not a bird herself, by nature of her mother's transfiguration, Hekate surely has much of the bird in her. As winged, creative inspiration, she promotes flights of the imagination.

Coo at her! Ask her to take you away with her to the land where images call to you, grab you, have their way with you, and transform your real life, where they produce through you all the fruit of your labor, all that nourishes you, Mother Earth.

Hekate: Holy Wingedness I

A REVERIE:

> *I am a screaming bird-girl. I am a screamer.
> Screaming makes me scream. I cannot get it
> all out. I try and try. There are long moments
> between screams sometimes, but the
> screaming screeching one always returns. I
> am ridding myself of the lie: A raven streaks
> the sky. Caw-calling.*

[Fig. 76]

Hekate's Crow

*Because of its black color, the crow is associated
with the idea of beginning, i.e., maternal night [and]
primogenial darkness. Because it is also associated
with the atmosphere, it is a symbol for the creative
demiurgic power. Because of its flight it is considered
a messenger. In classical cultures, it retains certain
mystic powers and in particular the ability to forsee
the future; hence its caw played a special part in rites
of divination. In Christian symbolism it is an
allegory of solitude. [In alchemy it stands] in
particular for the nigredo [and also for the]
separating out of the Elements, the putrifactio [both
of which conditions have a morbid quality attached
to them].[194]*

[Fig. 77]

[Fig. 78]

Shard 11: Crowdog-Girl and Hekate

a woman recalls:

Black crows bigger than cats lived outside my window. When I felt lonely, I would go to them. When I moved from Washington State where "home" was to Southern California, a crow lived outside my window on Orange Drive in Los Angeles; one lives outside in the tree where I live now, too. When I was a little girl and no one talked to me, crows did. They were my friends, like family. It was like going to the back porch to talk to brothers and sisters when I got lonely. I could hear the dogs call out, too; I would call back to them and then more dogs that I didn't know would call back to me.

I know this dog who sits at my left hand, who hears all the way to the meadow, over the run of the creek. But a part of me is crow. Crow-me sees from far off, from the innermost branch: solitary. She says a little, not too much. She clutches understanding like a branch but doesn't get too close.

If I listen, the crows and the dog guide me, keep me safe. Maybe they call out, "Don't go, don't go!" Then I have to wait until a better time.

Mom didn't like animals much. I felt worst about her not liking crows because they are friends with the wolf-dogs. I got mad at her for not liking the crows, as if she didn't like me either. She doesn't know what kind of animal I am.

I heard this story and knew Hekate was with us with her lone-wolf soul and her far-darting crow's eyes, the ones that fix in the head of a small girl and watch over her.

Hekate: Holy Wingedness II

MY BIRD-HEART FLIES WITH YOU. I SIT DOWN TO WRITE
this morning. Can't get started. Headache, look
through a field of research notes, and open this piece
to you with only the title.

Suddenly, I have the urge to write to Lynn, my
future sister-in-law. I begin on some Japanese paper,
palest lavender with purple cranes flying across it. I
don't know Lynn well. It's taken me some time to
voice my thoughts and feelings to her.

What is astounding about not beginning to
write my/our project today until just this moment is
that, clearly, though you are not often thought to be
a goddess of marriage, as a goddess of the
crossroads, you are the mother of the union of
opposites, and of the masculine with feminine
energies coming together. Surely, you preside over
the passage into union of the opposing energies of
husband and wife. Or perhaps they are not
opposing, not really, but exploding into each other
at the point of contact? And always you guard the
unseen road giving way to the unconscious and even
the unconscious in ritual, the mystery of marriage:
the poetry of one hand flying out to another. Like
birds: your Holy Wingedness.

[Fig. 79]

Hekate, My Hobby (horse)

we ride a fury across the
moon plowing furrows
deep into the fields of
night brows of hoary
clouds

long ago when our bond was
Sworn in the eye of the mother
Asteria's belly
you saw me only now have I
heard
your voice calling me

riding rivers of nightmares
onto daydreaming plains
pieces of you everywhere
kneeling beside something red i
swear to find you

—Shira Marin

AT FIRST I THOUGHT I WAS INSULTING YOU, HEKATE. I talked with embarrassment about my writing "our" project as a "hobby." Mentioning you to a friend, she smiled eagerly and said, "That sounds like a much better way to go on, because hobbies are those interests we follow most passionately, make time for, and can't wait to get on with." And, of course, she was correct. Hekate, you are my soul pleasure.

I enjoy looking up the most everyday sorts of
words in order to find out what is inside of them. I
couldn't resist looking up the word "hobby" in the
dictionary and realized that a hobby isn't only a
pleasurable pastime, it is also a little horse. It is your
horse, Hekate. I must add that it is also a nag! As in:
You nag at me to do your work, but then I give in
and ride you over a mountain of books, inky hooves
trailing for pages: a sometime child at play. Years
after the February day on which I wrote the hobby
poem, I found the following fragment from
Chaldean Oracles to Hekate:

> . . .*[it is possible] that you will see a horse
> flashing more brightly than light or a child
> mounted on the swift back of a horse, a fiery
> child or a child covered with gold, or yet
> again a naked child; or even a child shooting
> arrows, standing up a horse's back.*[195]

[Fig. 80]

Follow the Horse to
Mute Swan Deep

*Suffering is the fastest horse that can carry us
to completion.*[196]

—Meister Eckhart

EROS MOMENTS ARE THOSE MOMENTS OF NOt KNOWING
that prompt us into the greater unknown, the
psyche's realm, towards Hekate. Today is beginning
with that sense of things. I have no idea where to
begin except that my fingers are curling over my
keyboard, ready to tap into whatever insists on
expression. I am waiting. In a foreword he wrote
recently, Russell Lockhart noted that he just sat and
waited for the memory of his camera and
Michelangelo's David to surface, not knowing at all
that they would materialize. Eventually, in that
particular way that the psyche feels magical, these
images arose, the psychic connection made itself.

I want to find the connections in my work
within pieces and across them. How deeply and fully
can I do this? What kind of effort is called for:
sitting, letting go of preconception and judgment,
trusting the psyche to inform me The simplest way.
About very difficult things, it is often difficult to
become very simple.

My attention is pulled up the bookshelf; I notice
horse-egg-and-bird, which share in common a space
alongside the wiry Medusa that I sculpted in 1986.
These objects of nature in their proximity to the

stultified beauty of Gorgon belong together, but not because of their proximity.

The egg, the original home of the bird; Medusa's head, the home of the horse. Egg and head incubate new life. Bird and horse spring forth winged. And Fly. Free. The one way Gorgon can fly: through her winged horse-child, Pegasus. How the frozen feminine spirit can come to life again on the powerful haunches of winged instinct!

a reverie:

> *I know the frozen place. Its rough edge has scraped raw the borders of my being.*

But then Hekate appears:

a woman's reverie:

> *Elly, remember your horse, the one that lives at grandma's? That horse had to say goodbye to us while you were here at home. It couldn't wait, but it sent you a big goodbye with a hug before it left. I thought we could say goodbye, too, from here, maybe light a candle and say goodbye. Shall we do that together and wave bye-bye? Goodbye, sweet horsey, have a good journey!*

The mother who told me about her daughter and the horse may or may not have said "goodbye" with Elly, but I needed to. To say "goodbye" is to say, "God be with you." Saying "goodbye" is a way of connecting with something sacred, connecting with our divine nature, reminding and reattaching to that aspect of ourselves and others as we depart from the place in which we have dwelt. Maybe we can feel it together. When we say "good-bye," something of the divine passes between us; maybe here, too. Maybe we can make this deeper connection, after all, for Hekate's sake, to bring her beauty into outer expression.

Just writing of the intention to be connected with sacred life can affect the desire of the divine to reveal itself. In this moment, Hekate, you appear. It had to be you, Hekate, for this is your project, and you are the goddess of the horsepower of language that is image.

[Fig. 81]

SwanLike

IN THE MIDST OF THIS WRITING, THE IDEA FOR THE
name of my publishing company has come to me.
I have been drawing my initials unconsciously into
the form of a swan. The "s" is the body and the "m"
creates the feathers. Amazing to manifest my
connection with the swan, to see a swan in myself
when at times I see an ugly duckling. But I've always
loved "Swan Lake"; since girlhood I have thought a
swan was hiding somewhere in my life. Prayed for
transformation. The Swan Lake ballet is coming to
San Francisco any day now! Uncanny that the ballet
comes to town in the midst of this writing.

Hekate floats the swan's image to consciousness.
It is in her nature to transform, not from the surface
but from the depths. Where is she in the movement
from ugly duckling into swan's regal beauty? On the
human plane, the movement is parallel to Cinderella
of the ashes movinginto Cinderella at the prince's
ball. But the transformation comes from deep
instinct, from some inner aspect yearning for change,
yearning to become ourselves: creatures of beauty,
the beauty of the psyche in its myriad
manifestations.

Fair-faced and SwanLike:
The Graeae

THE GRAEAE, THE GRAY ONES, OF PIC-FATHER, HAD gray hair from birth and only one eye and one tooth among them. The Graeae belong to Hekate. Their name in the form "Graeci" means "worshippers of the Crone," this crone who was considered to be an earth goddess whose primary animal form is the sow.[197] The Graeae appear as a triad in the myth of Perseus and Medusa; they serve as guardians of the cave and Medusa. Unwittingly, they provide Perseus with their one seeing eye. That is, they provide for him the particular, needed crone- like feminine vision to make his way through the cave to Medusa—that is, into the Underworld. To consider the eye essential to this context, we have to consider Hekate's attributes related to magic, vision, language, and chthonic nature.

Important to this context is the sense of the Graeae's vision as paradoxical: "dark/light, old-young, ugly/beautiful, animate/inanimate" —containing the paradoxical, trickster-like nature that is Hekate's. The eye of the Graeae is said to be, in some accounts, magical, and enables the sisters to comprehend the tree alphabet in the forest that borders their home.

Together with the single eye, the Graeae's single tooth is divinatory and allows them to cut the alphabet letters from the trees in the forest.[198] I love Patricia Berry's fantasy of this eye and tooth:

Words that grow on trees. Letters, language,
words hidden in wood. . .matter's own
words... this eye that can read trees is
something to get hold of. It's like the origin
of mythical vision and speech, cut from
nature itself....

Berry speaks of Perseus' boarish, one-eyed thrust into darkness as compulsive—"narrow, urgent, and animal-like" —and immediate. The individual who has this perception *is* the eye. Tooth and eye, "that single straight perception, release an animal energy, an instinctual certainty where acting and perceiving are one thrust, like the boar."[199]

Not to be forgotten is the fact that with this perception, Perseus is related like the Graeae to an archaic sow goddess and a pig-father. He looks and acts in ways that contain both the human and the animal in proper balance, which is exactly what Hekate would have us do. As Berry says, his sensibility "is a dark, underworld perception, a psychic surety, a thrust not into the world but into darkness,"[200] Hekate's paradoxical darkness.

Come with me. Let's root around in the psyche, in Hekate's cove of wonder and woe, that place of becoming one with ourselves.

[Fig. 82]

In Reflection:

I FEEL AFRAID AGAIN; I EAT IN 3'S—CORN CHIPS; I
befriend fear. I see now what the swan is doing in me
and in my work, at least in part. It comes not
through the masculine rendering of Zeus as swan
but through that of the Graeae, connected with the
depth of the instinctive feminine mystery: the
Underworld swan, Hekate's swan. In fact, another
rendition of the Demeter-Persephone myth, depicted
at the Theban shrine of the Kabeiroi, shows water
birds (including swans) accompanying the goddesses
Demeter and the winged Hekate Angelos in their
search for the ravished Persephone.[201]

I pick up the dictionary, which actually fell open
to "swan"; popping off the page from the margin of
the *American Heritage Dictionary* was an
extraordinary picture of a *mute* swan, which I hadn't
heard of before, though I'd seen this swan many
times. There's the "m" word for my publishing
company. But then, aren't "mute" and "swan"
opposed or paradoxical in some way? "Swan" shares
the root "swen-" with the words "sound" and
"singer"—they are certainly not mute! These two
words together become a curious name for a
publishing company whose primary purpose is to
make sound on paper. Or is it that writing has no
sound? Or is it that swans are creatures of
unspeakable beauty—until they open their mouths?

Is this a judgment I pass on myself? If I proceed
in this way, a picture of conflict arises. But I have a
very positive attachment to the swan, and for good

reason as you will see. So, I dismiss the idea of this figure being negative. I hold the tension of the sense of the mute swan who, when she opened her mouth, would say something of value no matter her vocal quality. You will understand this idea if ever you have heard a swan's song! I want to know more about this mute swan and check not only my psyche but also the field guide to birds of North America:

> *Mute Swan: Cygnus olor—an old world species introduced into eastern North America and commonly seen in parks. It breeds locally in the wild. When swimming, neck is held in a graceful S-curve; the secondary wing-feathers are often raised. The dull rose bill of the immature is black at the base. Voice, a low grunt, is seldom heard (italics mine). Wing beats of flying birds produce a diagnostic hum.*[202]

As opposed to the tundra, whooper, or trumpeter swan, I trust that this mute swan is the one; it is the only swan whose neck is S-curved. More than that, it is the one who flew off the dictionary page.

But the muteness? Its voice is seldom heard. Is this my present, is it my conflict, or is it my future? Am I looking forward to a future of muteness or a swan in potentia? I don't fancy being transformed into someone who looks attractive either inwardly or outwardly, but who can't express herself. Hekate has come to indwell and to saturate our beings with her truth, reconciling forever masculine and feminine silence in words on the page or in some different nonverbal form altogether.

Popping up importantly now is the idea of the "singer" living in the swan. Is it that one song waiting to be heard before she dies: the swan song? Or is there singing going on always inside her, which is never heard by others but to which her own ears will always be attuned. There is not only singing in the swan, there is a swan in the singer, for that is the meaning of my name in Hebrew, the English translation of which is "Carol." This is the name that in childhood I wished had been mine instead of Patricia. Having gotten my name right after all—with the help of a rabbi—makes clear to me that the psyche intends to create its balance and does not cease in its expression along a particular path until it has done so. For this reason, primarily, I trust the psyche even when it takes longer than I think is reasonable. The downy underside of this outer-world expression is that only "priests and priestesses of Eleusis were looked upon as descendants of the dwellers of the air and the water, gods [goddesses] of the wind and the sea, and particularly of the swanlike "good singer."[203]

[Fig. 83]

Shh?

THIS EXPLORATION IS NOT ONLY OF PUBLISHING,
or out loud, and not only about making words sing
or fly; it is about grappling with the singer. It is
about keeping silent in spite of the instinct to sing
(irrespective of virtuosity). What creates transformation in both singing and writing? It is a voice
conflict; I voice my conflict. Does the swan worry
about whether its voice is adequate? No! It becomes
what it becomes with instinctive confidence. Without
question or analysis of intellect, like Perseus with the
gifts of the swanlike Graeae, it bores through with
tunnel vision, tooth and nail.

But what must be the connection? Is it a big
something, obvious, like those chunky Tinker Toy
knobs of child's play, so much in evidence? The
pleasure of child's play, that instinct, has something
to do with it. That is what I'm getting at. That
instinct is what I need to turn to, to make these vital
connections that are missing in and among Hekate's
pieces.

So let's start with instinct that glows, like the
photo of the swan in the *American Heritage
Dictionary*: a blazing white feathered body,
luminous behind a head and neck that are in the
foreground but cast in shadow; only the merest hint
of light haloes the swan's crown. Not much intellect
is needed for this project. The instinct to connect, the
urging light of the body, is needed in great measure,
however. The swan brings the instinctive message to
connect.

Instinct is that innate aspect of behavior that is complex and rich with potential, but depleted by society's dicta, even though instinct is normally adaptive. Instinct is a powerful motivation and an impulse as well as an innate aptitude. The word's meaning, which is thought to be obsolete, is timely to my soul and feels to me to move in the direction I am headed: impelled from within, imbued. The etymology reveals the rest: to instigate, urge on, prick, incite. See "steig-." I turn to the *American Heritage Dictionary* Appendix: To stick, pierce, prick, stitch, or sting; to thrust, puncture, separate, spur on, quench; tattoo, pointed, and tiger. And that which arises from instinct, i.e. instinctive, is deep-seated, inveterate, and spontaneous.[204] Clearly, instinct is not the thought of the intellect but the "thought" of the body that, urged on by the psyche, pierces consciousness. That which arises from and rides on the power of instinct is pointed toward connection, the arrow of the god Eros, shadowed by Hekate.

i dream a swan

i move steadily, smoothly down the runway.
i sit right by the window watching the other
planes strive for flight. That
moment when the wheels leave the ground is
magic: the duckling becomes a swan. i
wriggle my toes and push a long stretch
through my legs into the balls of my feet. It's
the feast of the new moon—Hekate's time.
Now in flight, i feel closer to her,
to the merest hint of a crescent telling her
presence.
A warm shudder rushes through my chest.

So, who is your animal familiar? Dream: Find
out. Dream again!

[Fig. 84]

Mute Swan Deeper

MUTE SWAN DEEP, DEEPER INTO THE DARK THAT IS AT once engulfing and impenetrable until she gathers the courage to pierce it: the dark that turns round itself into what? Down the hole like Alice into the body, into the gut of dark. What calls to the Mute Swan here? Does life beckon only to its darkness, never to see the light—never to grasp the security of wall, never to know the parameters of life's innards?

Mute swan, so close to the unspeakable, knowing it. Like the dark, what does it want from her, what is its need? From nowhere appears the coin bearing her image. In Ionia, Greece, they knew her. In 300-200 B.C ., they knew Keep. They grasped the unquestioned exchange of life. Like coins, Mute Swan sailed silently from one hand to another, from dark pocket to deep, dark pocket, appearing only in the light of exchange. That powerful moment when money talks. And so the Swan. The medium of exchange, from hand to hand, bridging continents of experience, not caring for church over brothel, regarding all matters equally.Her Holy Spirit is everywhere. Mute Swan meets it and is it. Moves with it, is moved by it. Dances it. Dances in the dark that becomes the light of the Holy Spirit. The ultimate Paradox is the Parclete, the Swan who changes into the Dove. To go into one's darkest depths to face oneself: ugly duckling shadow meets Holy Dove. Unspeakable Void becomes Amazing Grace. Two faces, one coin. Is this it—the fullness of

it? Amidst the depths of these words I cast about.
Somewhere in their psychic recesses must be my ugly
duckling, my Red Queen, my Mad Hatter, my
Cheshire Cat. But perhaps this time those characters
aren't the point. The pivot of Mute Swan's moment
is the Holy Paradox: Hekate.

[Fig. 85]

Pointing to the Agony of Life,
Death, and Rebirth

MIMESIS, TAKING ON HEKATE AS ARCHETYPE ELUDES ME
but, Hekate, I reach for you. These extraordinary
paradoxical words from T. S. Eliot in "The Four
Quartets" describe the path to you, the sense of you
repeating in the way the spiral returns to its circular
point but always at a deeper layer:

> *You say I am repeating*
> *Something I have said before. I shall say it again.*
> *Shall I say it again? In order to arrive there,*
> *To arrive where you are, to get from where you*
>   *are not,*
> *You must go by a way wherein there is no ecstasy.*
> *In order to arrive at what you do not know*
> *You must go by a way which is the way of*
>   *ignorance.*
>
> *In order to possess what you do not possess*
> *You must go by the way of dispossession.*
> *Inorder to arrive at what you are not*
> *You must go through the way in which you*
>   *are not.*
> *And what you do not know is the only thing*
>   *you know*
> *And what you own is what you do not own*
> *And where you are is where you are not.*[205]

All of Eliot's words reflect my sense of finding
Hekate again, that place in which we could meet, that

place beyond intellect, where the divine paradox manifests, and I somehow grasp it. This is also how I felt in my despair before I came at all to terms with the vast depth of Hekate's nature; I whirled in the wind of her paradox. Everything was true without discrimination. And just as I thought I understood something, had within my psychic grasp the essence of her veiled being, I could feel it slip away.

Even with a variety of experiences over several years, a strange need urges me still deeper, down further and into psychic spaces that I hadn't previously conceived in order to meet Hekate:

> *Here and there does not matter*
> *We must be still and still moving*
> *Into another intensity*
> *For a further union, a deeper communion*
> *Through the dark cold and the empty*
>   *desolation,*
> *The wave cry, the wind cry, the vast waters*
> *Of the petrel and the porpoise. In my end is*
>   *my beginning.*[206]

THE
IMPOSSIBLE
UNION...
RECONCILED

Hekate as Self: I

My work: The energy that fills me also binds me,
keeps me from expressing myself completely.
Hekate, you said you would protect me from her, the
big her, that other mother. You promised to keep my
eternal flame burning, that you would keep the inner
sanctum aglow with your immortal light. If you do
not burn inside, Sacred Wonder, I am lost. No
imagination I can have without your presence
touches the amazing beauty you bring to my sight,
to my life, when I am conscious of you beside/within
me. Seeing the world through the veil of your
perception is everything.

You are the Holy that I am, that we all are at
one with, truly, all one: This means we are one with
the profane, as well. (How many would consider this
mad? Countless?) But my trust in you, my personal
experience of yielding to your nature much larger
than my own, gives me courage. You are one who
resonates from the unknown faraway reach but
abides at hand. Some poets know it: T. S. Eliot and
Diane Di Prima, Robert Bly, Antonio Machado,
Holly Prado: How many I could name! The Native
Americans, so close at hand in our society, know this
place from where Hekate speaks. The alchemists
knew it: that relation between what is above and
what is below, that these oppositions are reflections
of each other in ever deepening hues, roiling in
endless time.

Each of us must find a sense of you, of
wholeness, of the Self that guides us with exquisite

acumen and accuracy and without harsh judgment. This sense of Self does not condemn. This Self includes all directions of experience—above, below, across; all dimensions of reality, inner and outer; the whole of nature, sacred and profane, refined and primitive, constructed and organic—all embodied in a living, ever-reeling spiral.

[Fig. 86]

Hekate the Destroyer

I'M CERTAIN NOW THAT THE DESTRUCTIVE HANDS OF the negative feminine figure who envies and spoils all within her grasp are not the same as those belonging to Hekate. The experience of working through The Spoiler turns out to be very instructive in helping me to discriminate Hekate, The Destroyer, from this other negative feminine character. Within Hekate's cyclic and paradoxical nature, her destructive act is performed in the service of creating something new, truly new. Imagine that!

Mother: Maw?

THE ETYMOLOGICAL TRUTH IS THAT TO BE DEVOURED IS also to be "entwined" or "embraced," that is, to enter into the mother's womb.

The poet Peter Levitt once said, speaking of Mother's Day and the joys of being a "Mamma's Boy," how important honoring his mother was to him. As he had grown in her womb, he considered her his first roommate! How can we hold an attitude that allows us to return to Mother openly and with love without getting caught in our personal mother experience; how can we see the larger Mother Hekate who stands guard deep within as our psychic core, protecting us as no outer-world mother can? May we all come to rest in the Mother Maw!

Primordial Time

PRIMORDIAL TIME HAS THE FORCE OF TIME NOW.
Primordial time brings life now; it is a generative
force.[208] That is what makes Hekate transformative
even as a death goddess, still and forever a
generative feminine power.

The Hint Half-Guessed,
the Gift Half-Understood
is Incarnation:
The Impossible Reunion Reconciled

TIME AFTER TIME I IMPLORE HEKATE TO REVEAL
herself as she did at the beginning of my journey
with her. Clearly, I need not have worried but only
waited actively; the proper moment for a new
revelation and Hekate's appearance have always
coincided. These moments Carl Jung called
"synchronicity"; Nathan Schwartz-Salant calls
them "fallout" from the realm of the archetypal.[209]
But one of my favorite descriptions of this journey
of worry and wonder at Hekate's visitations comes
from T. S. Eliot:

> ...*to apprehend*
> *The point of intersection of the timeless*
> *With time, is an occupation for the saint—*
> *No occupation either, but something given*
> *And taken, in a lifetime's death in love,*
> *Ardour and selflessness and self-surrender.*
> *For most of us there is only the unattended*
> *Moment, the moment in and out of time,*
> *The distraction fit, lost in a shaft of sunlight,*
> *The wild thyme unseen, or the winter lightening*
> *Or the waterfall, or music heard so deeply*
> *That it is not heard at all, but you are the music*
> *While the music lasts. These are only hints and*
>   *guesses,*
> *Hints followed by guesses; and the rest*

Is prayer, observance, discipline, thought
  and action.
The hint half guessed, the gift half
understood, is incarnation.
Here the impossible union
Of spheres of existence is actual,
Here the past and the future
Are conquered, and reconciled,
Where action were otherwise movement
Of that which is only moved
And has in it no source of movement—
Driven by daemonic, chthonic
Powers. And right action is freedom
From past and future also.
For to most of us, this is the aim
Never here to be realized;
Who are only undefeated
Because we have gone trying;
We, content at thelast
If our temporal reversion nourish
(Not too far from the Yew-tree)
The life of significant soil.[210]

[Fig. 87]

Inspired Symbiosis

REMEMBER. . .?

> *An unconscious longing for inspiration and ecstasy may well be characteristic of our age. We should at least permit ourselves these longings, even if we are no longer open to ecstasy itself. To be taken hold of by [divine nature] means to be possessed and to permit ourselves to be possessed. It signifies symbiosis rather than individuation. We often hear that mystics are able to establish a symbiosis with the divine without ceasing to individuate, having found a good rhythm between symbiosis and individuation. This balance can be explained psychologically by the fact that the more defined the ego boundaries are, the greater their permeability.* [211]

Certainly no mystic I, but Verena Kast's declaration heartens me. To move with Hekate's project and its demands to move in and out of archetypal reality? Kast's words evoke images of connecting with and expressing the potential of a divine child who could be comfortably symbiotic! RE-member: Not devoured by, entwined. Or maybe just in the Great Lap of. Or sitting in the shade of.

[Fig. 88]

Tangerine Mother:
Heart Home of Hekate

WAS I SEVEN OR EIGHT YEARS OLD ALL OF THOSE
TIMES when I was locked out of the house, that
supposed warm place of safe harbor that never felt
quite warm or safe? The discovery of no one home
terrified me and drove me to the far corner of the
lower garden behind the tangerine tree. I could be
safe there. The round green blossoms and its
fruiting smelled so pungent, felt so inviting and
nourishing. I loved the fragrant bitter spray that
numbed my tongue as I bit the peel to get the
orange flesh inside. I love my Mother.

[Fig. 89]

L's Tree-Mother

MORE THAN 10 YEARS AGO, BEFORE THE ADVENT OF Hekate's reappearance, a woman who was feeling very low came to visit with me for psychotherapy. As we worked together, she began to chip away at the blocked place that pressed her inside and pushed her away from seeing and becoming more fully herself. Intent as she was, a sense of herself and a possible connection with the psyche came into view. Increasingly, she looked for this relationship and found it to be dependable. Her discovery of her intuitive nature and feel for symbolic expression developed and began to enrich her life.

At about the same time, she decided to train as a marathon runner and one of her favorite routes took her along the Santa Monica palisades in Southern California. Her running took her much deeper, though, as she came to realize that she always passed by an enormous tree that, after a point in time, stopped her on every run. For her, the tree became irresistible. She found herself wanting to sit beside it, then nestle into it, to throw her arms around it. Finally, she began talking to it and asked it to help her with her pain. She came to the office most weeks talking about her "Tree-mother" and the warmth and sense of possibility she felt sitting next to her new mother, the one who wanted her to become fully herself. This Tree-mother became the deepest, most potent rootedness to this woman's unconscious life. And so it is.

Mother and child reunion

In modern psychological text:

> *In the foreground of joy stands the identity
> of the ego with the transpersonal Self, a
> convergence that enlarges the experience of
> the ego and enables it to open up and
> experience something unexpected. In the
> background is the experience of the divine
> child who dwells in the fullness of the
> positive mother archetype.*[212]

But let me say it again: From the beginning, in
ancient times, Hekate said:

> *Having spoken these things,
> you will behold a fire leaping skittishly like a
> child over the aery waves;
> or a fire without form, from which a voice
> emerges;
> or a rich light, whirring around the field in
> spiral.
> But [it is also possible] that you will see a
> horse
> flashing more brightly than light,
> or a child mounted on the swift back of a
> horse,
> a fiery child or a child covered with gold, or
> yet a naked child;
> or even a child shooting arrows, standing
> upon the horse's back.*[213]

HEKATE'S (OTHER) DAUGHTER

[Fig. 90]

Am I my Mother's daughter?

OTHER PARTS TO THIS DREAM FELL AWAY. ALL THAT IS left is the image of a very old woman wearing layer upon layer of black clothing: some delicate, some sheer like chiffon; some sturdy like wool, some strong but rich like velvet. I'm amazed. The woman belongs to herself and is oddly forceful—an elegant and dignified bag lady.

No doubt she is an image of Hekate, wandering, looking for a place to indwell. No doubt she is Hekate, fascinating those who see her, quickly exhorting them to take her in—into the home of their hearts, into their culture of being.

I dream:

> *I was getting ready to go on a movie set to work as an actress. I kept having to put on different clothes; it seemed I was putting on outfits on top of outfits. Clearly, I looked better in some than others. The last thing I remember trying on was a black jumpsuit with silver trim or polka dots or something, and it seemed to be padded in some way. It felt awkward to have it on over other clothes, but I probably would have looked good if I'd been wearing it by itself.*

I, daughter of Hekate
garbage-can-child

Hekate's Daughters:
Multiple Birth of a Movie

Roiling, raging under a blanket for the past
half-hour. Is there anything I can do to take away
the pain that is everywhere inside: my eyes-stomach-
right-shoulder-back-left-knee-inside-right-ear-left-
ring-finger-cuticle? My heart? It's really in my heart.
I feel lost, bereft, without a place to dwell. Like
Hekate. I am Hekate's daughter. I want something in
this darkness that won't leave me, that entraps me.
Hekate, help your daughter!

Nothing happens. I wait. My mind begins to
wander to last evening when Owen and I went to see
a documentary called "Hollywood Mavericks." As
we left the theater, we both noted the absolute
absence of female directors featured in this film: No
American female filmmakers of repute. Any female
director would have been a maverick by her
existence alone! I remember a dream I had in 1988
that I laughingly entitled "Hekate: The Movie." I
was titillated by the idea not only because I have
been in the industry but because film is image,
dynamic image, as is Hekate. Hekate is the goddess
of the image and of all that is visual. Although I have
felt intensely about the possibility of Hekate as a
movie, I have only thought about it minimally in a
practical way. I think of this film first as deepened
intimacy with Hekate and only then sharing her
revelation with others.

Until then, I shoot slides. I have some of people
and my dog, Ginger, that I really like. I've been
noticing that my ability to translate my vision

through the lens is developing. I would never have guessed this unfolding. When I photograph people, it works; it often works. It's an odd experience for me seeing beyond a flat image of someone and, instead, viewing human essence: attitudes, feelings, thoughts, world view. Like shooting through people. So, maybe the Arab people are right in saying that if one has one's picture taken, one's soul is captured by the photographer.

Good women, lend Hekate your souls; she will return them to you with her blessing. Some people seem to have a Hekatean essence. How I know this is my secret for the moment. But someday, you may see this collection and then you can tell me if you see or experience Hekate's presence.

I think of Margaret photographing her exhibit—all of the women in her family. It's dawned on me that I am not an only daughter. No, even now, lying alone at 4 a.m., I am not as alone as I first think. There are many of us. My sisters. And brothers, too, but they must wait for another time. I want now to stay just with these women, who for reasons that will become known in the film, are also Hekate's offspring. Their faces begin to flash across the screen of my inner vision. I feel extremely pleased by seeing who is there: Diane, Susan, Jane, Nancy, Jill, Holly, Ginger, Sooty, Betty, Suzanne, Marija, Sylvia. And then there's Kathy, Anna, Ann, Rose. And who else? Sophie, Margaret, others, and historically known figures no longer with us: Georgia O'Keeffe, Imogen Cunningham, Suzanne Valadon, H. D., Emily Dickinson, Sylvia Plath, Frida Kahlo. Stills. Photoscape. A movie. This dog can lie dreaming under the blankets. For now.

RE-CREATION

Meditation: Say It With Me

HEKATE, PASS THOUGH ME, AND MAKE THIS WORK WHAT it is to become. Hekate, pass through me, and make this work what it is to become. Hekate, pass through me, and make this work what it is to become. Hekate, pass through me, and make this work what it is to become. Hekate, pass though me, and make this work what it is to become. Hekate, pass through me, and make this work what it is to become. Hekate, pass through me, and make this work what it is to become. Hekate, pass through me, and make this work what it is to become. Hekate, pass through me, and make this work what it is to become.

Hekate, pass through this work, and make it what it is to become.

Hekate, pass through this work, and make it what it is to become.

Hekate, pass through this work, and make it what it is to become.

Hekate, Creative Storm, pass through me, and make this work what it is to become. Hekate, Creative Storm, pass through me, and make this work what it is to become. Hekate, Creative Storm, pass through me, and make this work what it is to become. Hekate, Creative Storm, pass through me, and make this work what it is to become. Hekate, Creative Storm, pass through me, and make this work what it is to become. Hekate, Creative Storm, pass through me, and make this work what it is to become. Hekate, Creative Storm, pass through me, and make this work what it is to become.

Sweet, Hekate, Goddess of eruption, the endarkening, the enlightening, pass through me and this work. Reveal yourself and bless all we are to become.

Hekate, Whirling Wind, pass through this work, and make it what it is to become.

Hekate, Whirling Wind, pass through this work, and make it what it is to become.

Hekate, Whirling Wind, pass through this work, and make it what it is to become.

Hekate at Summer Solstice

A DAY OR TWO AGO, I ASKED HEKATE WHERE SHE WAS at summer solstice. She answered lightly that she had been in my heart. I was shocked because I felt more alone than usual; she gave me no indication of her presence. But thinking back, Hekate is often not easily found. She, beneath the veil, if she chooses, can express herself as the gentlest balm of the season. You know, the one that wafts so softly, unnoticed as if that balm were not my very breath.

I Cast the I Ching:
The Abysmal

MY VISION SINKS INTO THE WATER. SOMETHING IS treading down under. Curious wonder. No excitement or euphoria, only settled, quiet joy: a half-hidden rock embedded deeply and solidly in a clear mountain river, the alchemical Lapis? The verdigris Shulamite of the "Song of Songs" is a woman seeking with veiled-green-eyes piercing the crystal surface of the river? Someone: She reveals herself just a little.

[Fig. 91]

Veiled Hekate

a woman dreams:

all of a sudden a whirlwind spun into view.
Inside it was a veiled woman in dark clothes,
tattered. Surrounding her was a soft, glowing
light. I wondered who it was. My lover thought
it might be you.
(I knew it was Hekate!)

a man dreams:

Hekate appears veiled in the
balcony of a church.

another man dreams:

a dark woman in red in a saloon type place is
hanging around a piano. She is alluring to me.
I try to resist her.
I can't. I am attracted to her.

The First Paradox of the Veil: the Bearable Being of Half-Light

She's not what she seems to be; there's more to her than meets the eye. That's what they used to say about me. (How often have I said this about Hekate.) Odd that these comments come back to me. Their truth shot through me then. Often I wondered about them; I came to no conclusions. I knew only that I was surrounded by something I had no image for. I kept my light under a bushel basket. That's how my mother would have put it. These many years later, I think of it as living my life under a veil. These are words that easily describe Hekate. I see now that I wasn't alone.

Under this veil, I know what is real. I know the challenge is to see directly. I know the challenge is to see not through the inherited eyes of family or research books but through the original eyes of my first sense of Self, Hekate's daughter under the veil— that one who underneath, underneath it all, is intensely curious, deeply playful, willing to get lost for the sake of adventure. Come with me. Come in. Come under the veil!

Hekate Hair and Glasses:
Paradox of the Veil 2

IT WAS BARELY 6 A.M. WHEN I FELT RUSTLED FROM SLEEP. But there she was, unexpectedly, in floating morning dress, just visible out of the triangular slit of that waking vision through which the world has only fuzzy, muted color. I practically laughed. I was certainly stymied by this sense of Hekate with her very long and shining dark hair combed over her face. She wore eyeglasses over her hair. Positively silly, yet I trusted she was serious.

What was the purpose or message in this behavior? This image was truly symbolic in the way it threw together disparate images to create something we'd generally not see in the course of daily life. This hairy view of life, of my work with her, veiled by archetypal femininity, and primitive at that, actually reminded me of being a child and never being able to keep the hair out of my face. No matter how hard I tried I was forever pinning it back away from my eyes, but only because my father had more than a few nicknames for me in my feral appearance. Didn't he see how hard I was working at peering through the heavy drape of locks like that sultry actress, Veronica Lake? Five-year-old-Shira: Woman of Mystery!

Back to reflecting on the moment: To put glasses over an obvious obstacle to vision is senseless unless I need to look with other eyes, with the vision of a feral child, a vision still in touch with a primordial reality. That child's eyes fix on instinct, and she only hid behind a veil of blue-black tresses in order to be found. Ultimately, parenting involves the play of instinct. Dear parents, please see me though the veil. Please!

As Foster Mother, Hekate would have done that for her child. Isn't that just basic Stone Age parenting? Isn't that animal husbandry?

Good parents, look at your children. See through their harried veils after long hours at school. See through their resistance. See the radiant vitality gleaming through bed-head coifs. How beautiful! There *is* a way to get through to them.[214]

I Haven't Long Today

To say "I haven't long today" doesn't mean that I can't begin. Even 20 minutes for Hekate is a must. Sometimes, it is all I can take of the creative storm she brings. But I *must* take it. I must take something of this gift given. My task here is to *embody* Hekate and to express her archetypal reality. I don't mean that I am Hekate; I am not identified with her, but my life on earth, by the same inexplicable turn as yours, belongs to the *anima mundi,* the world psyche—Hekate's womb, her Soul. This work is my homage, my tribute to the truth of her who lives within me. Hekate in all of us. Sometimes people have asked me why it is Her-in-me. My fate and my destiny, I think. Hekate herself constellates the poles of Fate and Destiny. There is no illusion, no delusion, but perhaps a projection. If it's a projection, then isn't the projection a reflection of what is meant to be acknowledged from within: the potential that wants to become real, the expression of Destiny?

Hekate: a vast archetypal terrain, too large for this human soul to embody. Her power and her intensity frighten me; I feel awe-inspired and cowed by her uprising. In light of her nature, what I can express is small. But clearly, I must follow this sense I have now of the importance of doing something small as opposed to doing nothing at all. Not honoring the small thing by giving it reality in the world squelches the creative impulse, and I, in turn, suppress Hekate's power to manifest her cyclic nature as the goddess of creation, destruction, and re-creation. More than two days suffering rage does not attach legitimately to any other person or thing or situation in my life, which tells me that this feeling belongs to Hekate. It is rage that erupts when I am *with* Hekate. Demanding, she challenges me, "What are you going to do about it?"

Diane of Hekate

SINCE 1988, SMALL EXPERIENCES HAVE BEEN LURING Diane and me toward our meeting with Hekate. Take the facts of my bodyworker friend having worked with Diane and my poet friend Susan having studied with her years ago; both have encouraged or nudged me now to speak with Diane. And most recently, Diane and I, unbeknownst to each other, have been studying simultaneously, though at different hours, with the same Italian professor. *In-cre-di-ble. Grazie!* Incredible? Hekate!

It's August of this year and, finally, time for some editorial feedback. The poet, Diane, says, "Yes." She has time to review the material. We meet, and though we have never really talked before, it is somehow between us like two Sicilian women who sit around a table in Palermo every afternoon paring apples and figs. Or maybe it is Hekate between us. Although extremely literate in the classics, Diane knows little of Hekate from formal research. But she knows Hekate *from experience*. I knew this before giving her my manuscript because I had read her *Loba* poems.

Emerson said that every word was once a poem. The words that make images, the words that make poems, and those who speak in this way belong to Hekate. Diane, the poet, belongs to Hekate. My sense of Diane, which includes the ties through Susan and Jill and the Loba poems, ultimately drew me to approach her.

Recording Hekate

AUGUST 31, 1991, 2 P.M.: TOGETHER, DIANE AND I huddle over the work. In response to Diane's question of whether to tape-record our conversation. I tell her that I do want to record this time together, so I don't miss a single piece, a shard, of the broken mystery. I want the hecatomb of shards—all of the pieces that belong to Hekate. I feel fierce about doing her justice; I want to render Hekate as she wants to be rendered or as I trust is her wish. For more than 2-1/2 hours we talk. Diane is even in disposition, clear-minded, but leaving room for the unexpected, serious in the moment but not without humor. I am astonished that my intuition about this conversation has born such bountiful fruit. But then this harvest is Hekate's; I am only the plow in her sacred hand. This time with Diane is special: She is the first woman I have allowed into the inner sanctum of my written work with Hekate; she is the woman Hekate wants as midwife for my labor.

At 4:30, we finish. Swollen with joyful possibility, I gather my belongings and leave. I'm going to take my dogs to the park so that we can revel in this late afternoon's glorious almost-autumn light. At home, I am snapped out of my reverie by a call from Diane, who tells me that I've left the tapes at her house and she'll be glad to send them to me. I trust her to send them, although I am struck with anxiety by my forgetfulness. These tapes feel so vitally important to Hekate's life; her present and future and my present and future are encased in these small plastic cassettes.

When I received them in the mail two days later, I vow to guard them. I caught myself in a rigid kind of posturing about the tapes, desperate in a way, even though I knew that I needn't be worried. Depositing them on my writing desk so I could keep an eye on them, I went about what had become a busier schedule than I normally keep. The last thing I remember was taking the package to the car, where I intended to give the tapes a first listening. When I returned home, I scooped up the tapes with my armload of belongings and that was the last I ever saw of them. I cannot clarify whether they were misplaced thrown away, or…. I know only that they are still always on my mind, that even though Diane and I spoke again, those tapes, what they represent and what happened to them, are special in some ways I need to discover but may never know completely, for the meaning is veiled by archetypal reality: Their loss feels related to Hekate.

This is not the first time that something involving cassette tapes has gone awry for Hekate and me. Two other series of consultations were virtually inaudible, garbled, or without a sufficient sound level, although these factors had been accounted for. With the third and most serious occasion of this kind occurring, I felt not only aggrieved but mystified. What was there in these losses that spoke "Hekate"? Was she behind the loss? Did she wish to remain that invisible, that veiled? If so, why then would she have me write the book? It was clearly time to get down to concretely organizing the material in such a way that the tapes would be particularly helpful. Could Hekate have intended this mysterious occurrence? If so, to what purpose? What was I out of touch with besides the tapes, and was their loss necessary for me to connect again or for the first time with something I was missing, perhaps even without knowing it?

Suddenly it came to me: The loss is a loss of connection, of eros, and not just any eros. I am suffering the loss of eros between mother and child that exists in the seeds of these words between Hekate and me and Diane. They are not to be born into the world, at least not in the film I had anticipated. Yes to Diane as midwife. Yet any gestation of the words must come through Hekate working through me.

I think of attributes of Hekate's that relate to this experience. She is a queen of paradoxical intention, a trickster in her own right, a riddle. That is, she both does and doesn't want these tapes to be heard, just as she wants both to be seen and unseen. The resolution of the question of visible Hekate is that she wants veiled-ness, to be seen—sort of! She wants an aspect of her privacy, her sacredness, her mystery to be preserved. In this, she is a lesson to us all. In this world where all is out front, so direct, Hekate stands for the sense of instinctual femininity that knows better! She stands for indirection that may be a subtle form of directness, too subtle for the present age but necessary to discovering life as a whole and our inner lives in deeper layers.

In Hekate's Cave

I HAVE MOVED BEYOND LAZINESS NOW, ONTO THAt landscape where psyche is alive, that place where Hekate dwells. It is the deep and lonely place, that cold cave of autumn that burrows under the earth into which I plunge to meet her in her darkness. She wants my words. I stay with her, not lifting my hand from the page on which I honor her name. There is no way out of this cave until Hekate is ready to have me leave. My life is lived in an underworld in which nothing is possible that is unrelated to Hekate's work of revealing the hidden and veiling the too much seen.

Hekate in her burnished robes is the goddess of autumn, of all things—like her ripening, harvested, then driven underground. She is goddess of the time *between*, before a clear sense of direction arises, of the borders of consciousness, the psychological border line. Hekate presides over the conflict between staying above ground in the day-lit world with the warmth and comfort of solar clarity, where the daughters of Helios thrive, and going down into the realm where only the light of the psyche is shining, though sometimes darkly like the one-eyed Graeae and the Cyclops. The inner eye that restores wholeness visits in strange ways.

I vow to finish Hekate's book.

DARKENING
OF THE
LIGHT

We Cast the I Ching

36 *CHANGING TO* 49: *DARKENING OF THE LIGHT.*
My inner world is rumbling. I feel struck with the
quaking anxiety that arises in surrendering to
Hekate's desire to indwell not only in my heart. She
is the soul of my heart. In fact, she wants to be seen
as the soul of all of our hearts, the soul of the
world's heart—and rightly so, for she is the truest,
deepest, most feminine quality that we unwittingly
discarded millennia ago. Remember, indwelling
contains within it the quality of permanence.
Hekate is alive permanently in the tissues of our
hearts and souls. So just now, she wants conscious
indwelling. She wants us to know she is there, has
always been there. We have yet to allow her in, to
connect with her, to experience eros with her. I
have felt so struck by the magnitude of this
quaking inside that I cast the ancient Chinese
oracle, the *I Ching.* I ask Hekate to help me look
deeply into the words that arise in the casting:

> Hexagram #36—*Ming I—the Receptive, earth,*
> ` *the Clinging, fire*

> Judgment: *"In adversity it furthers one to be*
>   *persevering."*
>   *Remain steadfast.*

> Image: *". . .She veils [her] light, yet still shines."*

> *6 in the 4th place: [She] penetrates the left side*

of the belly. One gets at the very heart of the
darkening of the light, and leaves the gate
and courtyard.

Dissatisfied with my slowness in shaping
Hekate's book, I push for change, to move ahead, to
finish. The Sage points out that our inner light
darkens when we view difficult conditions through
the ego's eye and callow heart. But the power of the
Creative Impulse responds only to selflessness, to
letting go of the ego's vision. Give up my urge to
make visible progress? Give up my frustration? Yes!
Am I moving towards the heart of darkening,
towards its innermost secret sentiment? There is no
progress in following the wrong path. Swing to the
opposite reality: Do nothing but wait and watch.
Then:

Revolution/Molting

Hexagram #49 – Ko　　　　*the joyous lake*
　　　　　　　　　　　　　　the clinging, fire

Fire and water: an opposition of tendencies
that can destroy each other. Or will they only
subdue each other?

But—

Judgment: "On your own day you are
believed. Supreme success furthering through
perseverance. Remorse disappears.

Can I believe that change is now possible? The original sense of the Chinese character for this hexagram is an animal's pelt that changes in the course of a year by molting. Shed the outer until the bare essentials are revealed, until I see the heart, can get at it, touch it, hold it. Can I move to the limit of my abilities to express Hekate's reality?

Image: The superior man sets the calendar in order and makes the seasons clear.

I prepare for change almost unconsciously. Active revolution is insisting on conscious steps. Meaning? Have heart: Take courage; trust the Unknown even as I am moving into those still-to-be-crossed depths. Like magic, a flickering fire of order, but fluid. Not rigid. The seasons of my fear, pride, and self-doubt only burden my back. I let the weight of these fall away, at least for the moment. Joyous lake.

Moving Forward

The deep parts of my life pour onward, as
if the river shores were opening out.
It seems that things are more like me now.
That I can see farther into paintings.
I feel closer to what language can't reach,
With my senses, as with birds, I climb into
the windy heaven, out of the oak, and in the
ponds broken off from the sky my feeling
sinks as if standing on fishes.[215]

—Rainer Maria Rilke

[Fig. 92]

Crossing the Great Water II: Deep Crossing

Let the soul be a swimming animal
Let it scrape the bottom. Breathe
Water until it grows gills.[216]

—Frances Mayes

I STAND FAR FROM THE DUSTY SHORE, NO LONGER STARE into the foamy ruffle of the water's edge. The first shock of toes plunging into icy water has worn away. My body has long ago grown accustomed to the freshness of the shoals. Only my head averted to the horizon declares me a land creature; my hair falls around the mounds of my all but submerged shoulders, sea grass floating on the salty surface. It happens again and again with the surge, that odd feeling of my bare toes barely touching the silty bottom. Grounded. Not grounded. Grounded again. This is my last chance to turn back, but I cannot!

The next step becomes the swish of a tail fanning the current, propelling me; slicing fins steer the course. Headed where? How does the fish know where to go in the vastness of its journey across the great water? It instinctively knows the right direction, what comes next, what follows from what.

So, where is this journey leading me? How do I move through the deep water of this work with no landmarks, no compass? I am so into it my feet no longer connect with the soil of earthly reality. I have been treading water, but now I see that like the fish I need to dive down into deep blue in order to cross over, to overcome the obstacles of swimming at the surface. The work is carried by the wisdom of the deep, by the life of the Underworld. But how do I read the signs? The fish knows what to look for; it avoids danger and finds the best course. The fish is my compass. I let the fish move me; it is my guide!

Consider: I am in another moment of "not knowing," what Russell Lockhart calls an "eros" moment, that interval of having to respond to something not previously encountered from some place not previously known and so unrelated to. There is nowhere to go but deeper. Immersion into blue-black. Will something come to meet me? An underwater/ Underworld guide? Hekate? But in what form? In which of her many forms?

Hekate: She is the flow and the current of this water in the same way that she is the thrust under the arrow of eros, the underside of eros, that wanton instinct that rushes forward and "brings together" and "couples" entities, aspects, and people—against all logic. Desire colliding with desire. Where is that experience now? I am coming to meet, but who or what will come to meet me to link us more securely together? I move forward, all alone, feel the cold aloneness, scanning, waiting, full of the urge to open. Stay open. Stay in that place where something unexpected] can materialize and permeate, pierce, and penetrate me.

Hekate Where I Find Her: A note from the I Ching, Hexagram 64

". . .the transition from disorder to order is not yet completed."[217]

Materializing:

I watch Hekate's restoration as it occurs. This is the essence of my written effort: to make a dwelling place for Hekate to manifest in the everyday-ness of postmodern-life-on-earth. Put another way, I want to show my vision of the interaction of Fate (of which Hekate is Hellenic Goddess) and Destiny. This trajectory of my Life calls me to live fully through its cycle to an end that is currently veiled. And this, I firmly believe, is what is meant by *Living the Mystery.*

The I Ching, Gua #64 again:

Perseverance furthers! Move with it and cross the great water. This is my task before completion.

I interact with what is, like Fate, beyond control, and dance in the lunar light of Hekate's being. As Fate, she beckons me to join the mystery dance of Eleusis. Go to the preserved Villa of Mysteries amidst the ruins of Pompeii to see the frescos of Demeter and Persephone being reunited by Hekate. It is the Tenth Day.

Like Demeter and Persephone, we have danced and laughed in death and grief; we do so for joy, reborn, relieved. I do not have to stop; the music of words has just begun to pour forth with the sweetness of grapes at first harvest. Water-into-wine sacrament. Dionysus on the horizon. Renewal of instinctive life. The arising of Hekate.

The Cauldron

"NO" MOMENTS. "YES" MOMENTS. THE SAME
moments, stirring. Again, Hekatean paradox.
Turn to it, to what is. Fingers set to typing keys in
willingness; setting fingers to keys brings the
change, makes visible Hekate's *Ting*, the cauldron.
The cauldron brings supreme good fortune. New
Sacrament: We stir ritual nourishment to sacrifice,
to all-embracing sacredness.

Hekate, embodiment of the 3 Fates, exerts the
force of Necessity that governs Destiny. I cannot
avoid you, don't want to avoid you. And
ultimately, it is you who bring about the
harmonious confluence of Fate and Life. You are
no less than all of Life in its universe of cycles and
the magic of Fate and Destiny that harmonize in
synchronicity. I go, go deeply. Stir the cauldron!
Images, arise!

[Fig. 93]

Piercing:

Clearly, the dream is not a herald of
reflection's realm. It is an arrow of Eros.
There is little reason to grasp. Perhaps trying
"to grasp" is itself the wrong impulse.
Dreams do not seek reason's grasp but seek
another kind of touch....[218]

—Russell A. Lockhart

Is a dream's touch piercing as in the arrow of Eros?

Permeating:

DUENDE: EXPRESSING HEKATE IN ART.
Federico Garcia Lorca was certain that the muse and
the angel come from the outside. He wrote that "the
angel gives light, and the muse gives forms" to our
creative impulse. He did not know of the dark angel
and a dark muse who come from the depths and
belong to Hekate. But he knew something very
special of what comes from another place, "from the
remotest mansions of the blood." It can be described
by only one Spanish word: *duende.* As you read
Lorca and others below, you can't forget Hekate:

All that has black sounds has duende.[219]

Black sounds are the mystery, the roots
fastened in the mire

The duende, then, is power. . .is a struggle,
not a thought.

The duende is not in the throat. It crawls up
inside you, from the soles of your feet, an old
maestro of the guitar.

It is not a question of ability, but of true,
living style, of blood,
of the most ancient culture, of spontaneous
creation.

[It is] a mysterious power which everyone
senses but no philosopher explains.[220]

Lorca said that there are no maps, no
disciplines, to help us find duende. But duende
"burns the blood like the poultice of broken glass
. . .exhausts. . .rejects all the sweet geometry we have
learned [and] smashes styles." Duende wants not
forms but the marrow of forms. "Duende's arrival
always means a radical change in forms." Do you
hear the energy of Hekate here where our human
soul inflames with life, grips the flesh, and screams,
"Come alive"?

Listen to the singer La Nina de los Peines:

She had to rob herself of her skill and
security, send away her muse and become
helpless, that her duende might come and
deign to fight her hand to hand. And how
she sang!

Her voice was no longer playing. It was a jet of blood worthy of her pain and sincerity.

I think this image must be of Hekate herself:

Years ago, an 80-year old woman won first prize at a dance contest in Jerez de la Frontera [Spain]. She was competing against beautiful women and young girls with waists as supple as water, but all she did was raise her arms, throw her head back, and stamp her foot on the floor. . .Who could have won but her moribund duende, sweeping the ground with its wings of rusty knives.[221]

And imagine Hekate, attending the 17th-century Marbella, dying in childbirth in the middle of the road:

The blood of my insides is covering the horse. The horse's hooves throw off black fire.[222]

Duende does not come unless death is possible:

The duende must know beforehand that [s]he can serenade death's house and rock those branches we all wear, branches that we do not have, will never have, any consolation.

*With idea, sound, or gesture the duende
enjoys fighting
the creator on the rim of the well. . .The
duende wounds.
In the healing of that wound that never
closes lies the invented
strange qualities of [one's] work.*

*The duende draws near places where the
forms fuse together into a yearning superior
to their visible expression.*

*The duende. . .where is the duende? Through
the empty arch comes a wind, a mental wind
blowing relentlessly over the heads of the
dead, in search of
new landscapes and unknown accents; a
wind that smells of baby's spittle,
crushed grass, and jellyfish veil, announcing
the baptism of newly created things.*[223]

Hekate as Self

Penetrating:

LORD PENTLAND DIED. AS AN EXTRAORDINARY TEACHER of spiritual practice, my teacher, Lord Pentland prepared us, prepared me for something I could not glean on my own. He encouraged me to hold the tension between my sacred and profane natures, to grasp the deepest sense of the alchemical aphorism, "as above, so below," and to nurture within myself and for others a profound quality of compassion. Like all great teachers, he spoke of the most profound matters with the lightest touch and often with humor. I just noticed now, so long after that February day more than 30 years ago the importance of his death in my life. Lord Pentland had such an uncanny ability to turn the key on the exactly needed thought at the precisely right moment and to open that door to that other world to which we each strove for relationship.

Upon LP's death, my sense of belonging and my spirit plummeted. I don't remember ever feeling so bereft and lost. Something of the kind of "lost" that I felt when my father died: In my still 10-year-old's way, I recall myself asking, "Who will guide me; where can I turn now?" LP had left us a legacy of perspective: a sense of life much larger than any I had known before I met him. Others must have known what LP knew. The truth for me then and now is that somehow the particular expression of objective quality that Lord Pentland lived, his grasp of Life beyond the ego, did not appear in anyone else, or at least I felt no resonance. Had I not truly received anything of the experience of the Other consciousness I was struggling toward? I thought I might have come to some small experience in myself of this Other quality of existence, but could not make a new connection with a teacher. Had he not passed the experience of Objective Reality on to someone? No one seemed able to stand in his shoes. Actually, he never wore shoes indoors, only house slippers. I liked the fact that we had that idiosyncrasy in common; it made me feel that we had the same sense of life lived on the ground, in the dirt.

LP loved Rilke; he introduced me to Rilke. He grasped Rilke's connection with the sacred sense of life that, after a point, became a vision for my life. Rilke's quote about images is so Hekatean; I quote it to this day:

> You must give birth to your images.
> They are the future waiting to be born.
> Fear not the strangeness you feel.
> The future must enter you long before it happens.
> Just wait for the birth, for the hour of the new clarity.[224]
> —Rainer Maria Rilke

Upon LP's death, my spirit sank but kept struggling to stay afloat; my soul sank deeply into an abyss of grief. But Lord Pentland had led me silently to Hekate. He had prepared me to meet her, an event that occurred not long after his death. He may not have known this in a specific sense, but he forever wanted us to notice ourselves, our preconceived ideas, our automatic way of being-in-the-world, and to shed these to become ready for the unexpected.

Today, I would say we are becoming ready for the spontaneous arising of the psyche, learning to put inner quiet in the service of the psyche's voice—the psyche's "chorus of voices," as Russell Lockhart would say. If, as with the Chaldeans and the Neo-Platonists, to say "psyche" is actually to say "Hekate," then to come back again to an inner quiet place is to make way for Hekate to speak. If you know this experience, maybe you call your voice by some other name. Of most importance is that Hekate is seen in the archetypal background in the shadow of the names you call. You will recall, she is *Polymorphus,* the Many-formed.

I am dumbstruck now by the reality that I needed some kind of external guidance. I needed Lord Pentland to learn what is meant in us to *come as an organic sense of ourselves*, a whole sense that always involves the necessity of turning to a reliable *inner* sense of life; this inner guide embodies and validates the paradox of the instinct to sacred life and to the sacred life of instinct.

P.S. "Oh, yes, here is where the image of C. G. Jung's *Self* also surfaces," some might say: This *Self* is the meta-psychological construct expressing the union of opposites that is a totality of one's personality. Yes, the external teacher became the internal one; whatever LP offered came also and more deeply from Hekate! Hekate is the Whole that contains the secret center.

[Fig. 94]

From a Mortician's Daughter

SWEET WOMAN GODDESS HEKATE, MY TEACHER,
beyond religion, beyond spirituality, beyond Father
Fitzgerald and Sister Catherine Marie, beyond Mr.
Ellis and Naomi Katz, Ph.D., beyond Lord Pentland
and C. G. Jung, you will never die! No one will ever
see you with peaceful, red, waxen lips, holding one
flaming rose. No one will see you lying in a black
casket with silver fittings and pillowy white satin
inside. You will never die, Hekate. They cannot bury
you. You are my teacher eternal!

*Easy is the descent to Avernus: Night and
day the door of gloomy Dis stands open;
but to recall thy steps and pass out to the
upper air, this is the task, this is the toil!*[230]

—Virgil

END
PIECES

Poetry is about the divine.[225]
—Natalie Goldberg

Don't Come to Me with the Entire Truth

Don't come to me with the entire truth
Don't bring the ocean if I feel thirsty
nor heaven if I ask for light;
but bring a hint some dew,
a particle as birds carry
drops away from the water,
and the wind a grain of salt.[226]

POEM AS IMAGE IS A PIECE OF ETERNITY, OF DIVINE LIFE:
a piece of Hekate. See how she governs in Olaf
Hauge's demand to leave something in order to
remember the truth, a truth held back, not yet to be
told, linking something left unsaid and something
still to be said. Bring pieces, the hint, a shard of the
whole. In a sense, poems are veiled reality, meant to
draw us in, under, searching for the depths of them,
allowing us to immerse in the psyche of them. That
sense of hint and lure into the mystery are what
makes them of Hekate. So perhaps I cannot bring
you all of Hekate. True to her veiled nature, she
remains partly unseen. Just hinted at, like the deep
reality of poetry. An odd delight permeates me as I
read a recent note from Holly Prado Northup:

I've been dipping in to Robert Graves again
this afternoon, and he absolutely connects
Hekate with the White Goddess, who is the
muse of poetry, which [Graves] insists is the

moon herself in her various phases. She is everywhere:
everything, nothing, all as it shatters, and the ultimate One.

Oh, how I wish Mr. Graves, Hekate, and I could sit over a cup of hot English tea together!

Mono-poly-pan Hekate: Goddess for a Post-Postmodern Age

THROUGH SO MUCH OF MY WRITING WITH HEKATE, SHE has been the only one, the goddess; all other deities have stood in the shadow of her power. Often, I have considered that they were a mere splinter of her divinity; no other god existed in his or her own right, monotheism by another name. But now, I am clearly of another mind.

Following the contemporary philosopher and author Rodney Collin, everything has its own level of intelligence in one form or other; all things are in some way reflective of divine life and have a particular degree of consciousness. Hekate is the most potent image of this capacity that humans have to reflect and to increase consciousness. Hekate is the constellated embodiment of our whole humanness in this way, as it has progressed from the dawn of humankind. By this, I am considering the time from our diffuse whole consciousness to the atavistic fear and instinct that drove men to their fear and repulsion of the natural feminine traits bred in them. As a survival tactic, women capitulated to the ways of patriarchy and, finally, to the tyranny of the Patriarchy over us all, men and women alike.

The Patriarchy, as an archetype, became overdetermined. Hekate's arrival has evoked a dawning of this understanding in me. We have had as much masculine atomistic parsing of life and psyche as we need for our ego's development. It is now time for us to re-view our atavistic fears—those that drove the glorious Hekatean aspects of the Feminine Principle into the abyss of unconsciousness.

We will destroy ourselves unless we re-cognize and embrace these aspects wholeheartedly and soulfully, unless we re-member the mind- body, the spirit-instinct that is innate to us. We must restore Hekate and all she brings if we are to survive. If we wish to make true and lasting change, we cannot leave out the essential pieces that create change that are already natural parts of us: the primary one being compassion expressed in the desire to openly see, listen, and take in the reality of others. If we are to grow in consciousness, there is no other way. If we do not, we ultimately block the potential for personal and collective peace as well as the process that nurtures it between and among us.

What Kind of Spiritual Femininity

CHARLENE SPRETNAK, SCHOLAR AND WRITER, NOTED IN an early postmodern essay that:

> [the] goal of feminist spirituality has never been the substitutionof Yahweh-in-a-skirt. Rather, it seeks, in all its diversity, to revitalize rational, body honoring,

*cosmologically grounded spiritual
possibilities for women [and men].*[227]

My honoring of Hekate here accords wholly
with Ms. Spretnak, but in the spirit expressed by the
poet Muriel Rukeyser, she says that if one woman
told the truth about her life, the world would split
open.[228] Ms. Rukeyser's comment describes an
epiphany of Hekate. Telling the truth brings Hekate.
In its small way, this work is my earth quaking and
splitting, my invocation to Hekate.

Ultimately, perhaps we need no figures—"a
goddess myth without a goddess," as authors
Cashford and Baring put it. But I think that must
wait until the deities of our Western Culture have
consciously reclaimed parts of ourselves. It must
wait until we have recollected and humanized all
that we have projected onto the world, specifically,
our dark instinctual nature in its many-formed
manifestations. Hekate is a major figure in that re-
collective effort. My meanderings are meant to remind us all of that and of her as we dream the
dream onward. That is, to:

*. . .dream of the possibilities of our 'ancient
future,' some rapprochement between what
we are and what we can be.*[229]

—Diana di Prima

*Easy is the descent to Avernus: Night and
day the door of gloomy Dis stands open; but
to recall thy steps and pass out to the upper
air, this is the task, this is the toil!*[230]

—Virgil

[Fig. 95]

Every Poem, an Epitaph

THE END OR THE BEGINNING OR SOMEPLACE IN
BETWEEN:

> . . . *What we call the beginning is often the*
> *end. And to make an end is to make a*
> *beginning. The end is where we stand from. .*
> *We shall not cease from our exploration*
> *And the end of all our exploring*
> *Will be to arrive where we started*
> *And know the place for the first time.*[231]
>
> —T. S. Eliot

Eliot's words reverberate through these writings
because the voice of Hekate's being is alive here as
she holds the opposites, in her cyclical, constellated,
and paradoxical nature; her inspiration materializes
in Eliot's imagery. Every experience of image is a
vision of Hekate, marking the process for all
journeys, their beginning and their end, as she did
with Persephone. As the goddess of death, she
companions us into the Underworld, through it, and
brings us from the unknown to another unknown,
but renewed. We die and transform, but Hekate and
her vitality as creative life force does not die. She has
been hidden and forgotten, but she cannot die, not
even in her manifestations from prehistory, not in
her images in these modern times, certainly not
within our human psyches.

Hekate has no conclusion in Eliot's sense of
concluding. And so this work cannot end with

conclusions, with opinionated remarks that bind Hekate into the smallness of denotative definitions. Hekate is far too nuanced in her capacities for such confinement; to attempt such facile squeezing would yield only a false sense of Hekate's reality in us, personally and collectively. So Hekate is no neat package; she is not even an ancient vessel perfectly restored. Her imperfection of form is her perfection in nature. In her paradoxical wholeness, it is Hekate's nature to remind us, through our suffering and every small death, that she is actually present with us, within us as an unseen though not missing piece within our psyches—and therefore, she truly completes us. We suffer and *feel* incomplete and broken by not recognizing this. At the same time Hekate reminds us of our brokenness, she also reminds of us of restored whole humanness, even if imperfect. Yes, this is our archetypal heritage: that includes brokenness together with restoration that expresses human wholeness that we are *always*. Hekate reminds us that our human goal and evolution depend on continually grasping this sense of wholeness, being always present, remaining conscious of this fact.

Hekate shows us nostalgia, the pain of wanting home, and of reaching for and nestling into her divine, unconditionally accepting embrace. We will suffer until we accept this unseen part of ourselves. We must work at truly restoring Hekate in ourselves and in the world, until her image in us is clear and her vitality sates our hunger for all she can give us psychologically, through the soulful liveliness of images, manifest within ourselves or the world around us.

Each time we come to a new possibility, to the end, to an impasse, to feeling lost, not knowing which way to turn or to whom to turn—every time we come to a crossroads within or without—we come to Hekate, who will guide and companion us if consciously engaged. And so in honor of Hekate, the grand continuance between Life and Death, as the great mythologist Betty Smith put it, this writing ends with an epitaph that is an invocation:

> . . .*any action*
> *Is a step to the block, to the fire down the sea's throat*
> *or to an illegible stone: and that is where we start. We die*
> *with the dying: See, we depart and go with them.*
> *We are born with the dead:*
> *See, they return and bring us with them.*[232]
>
> —T. S. Eliot

Onwards, sideways, and down!

Notes

Introduction

[1] Carl Jung, *The Red Book*, Philemon Foundation and W. W. Norton & Co., 2013.
[2] Marianne Williamson, Return to Love: *Reflections on the Principles of A Course in Miracles*, 1992.
[3] James Hillman, *ReVisioning Psychology*

---

[1] James Hillman *Re-Visioning Psychology,* Spring Publications, (New York: Harper & Row, 1975), 3.
[2] Erich Neumann, *The Great Mother,* (Princeton, New Jersey: Princeton University/Bollingen Foundation/Mythos books, 1972)
[3] Carl Jung, *The Red Book,* (New York: Philemon Foundation and W. W. Norton & Co., 2009), 201, 208.
[4] *Ibid.*
[5] Marianne Williamson, *Return to Love: Reflections on the Principles of a Course in Miracles,* (New York: HarperCollins, 1992), 192.
[6] James Hillman, *Re-Visioning Psychology,* 12. *op. cit.*
[7] *Ibid.*
[8] *Ibid.*
[9] Joan Halifax, *The Fruitful Darkness, (*New York: Grove Press, 1993). This book in its entirety speaks of the feminine quality of life that must be restored within us to allow our recognition of our wholeness.
[10] Leonard Cohen, "The Future," Columbia Records, 1992.
[11] Futurity.org/globally-1-in-13-suffers-from-anxiety; healthline.com/health/depression/facts-statistics-infographic#2.
[12] Russell Lockhart, *Psyche Speaks: A Jungian Approach to Self and World,* (Everett: The Lockhart Press, 2014), 52.
[13] *Ibid.,* 52.
[14] James Hillman, *The Dream and the Underworld, (*(New York:, Harper & Row, 1979), 39, 59.
[15] Carl Jung, *Memories, Dreams, Reflections,* (New York:, Vintage/Random House, Inc., 1961), 192-193.
[16] Patricia Dale-Green, *The Archetypal Cat,* (Zürich: Spring Publications, 1983), 156.
[17] Betty Smith, Seminar, 1988.
[18] Joseph Conrad, Preface to *The –igger of the 'Narcissus,': A Tale of the Forecastle (*New York: Dodd, Mead and Company, 1897).
[19] Samuels and Samuels, *Seeing with the Mind's Eye, (*New York: Random House, 1975), xii.

[20] William Yabroff, *The Inner Image,* (Mountain View: Consulting Psychologists Press, 1995), 43.

[21] C. G. Jung, *Psychology and Religion: East and West,* Vol. 11, (Princeton New Jersey: Princeton University Press, 1969), 5364.

[22] Betty Smith, Seminar, 1992.

[23] William Shakespeare, "Macbeth," ii, l, 12.

[24] *Ibid.*

[25] *Ibid.*

[26] Sarah Iles Johnston, *Hekate Soteira:Study of Hekate's Role in the Chaldean Oracles and Related Literature,* (Atlanta, GA: American Philological Association/Scholars Press, 1990) 1.

[27] Hesiod, *Theogony,* (New York: Penguin Classics, 1973), 36-37.

[28] James Hillman, *The Dream and the Underworld, (*New York: Harper & Row, 1979), 40.

[29] Sarah Johnston, *Hekate Soteira,* 85, 112. *op. cit.*

[30] Rainer Maria Rilke, *Letters to a Young Poet,* (New York: W. W. Norton and Co., 1993).

[31] James Hillman, *Sulphur Anthology,* (Upsilanti, Michigan: University of Northern Michigan, 1996), vol. 16, 58.

[32] Joseph Joubert: brainyquote.com/citation/quotes/quotes /j/josephjoub121637.html#2166lGHIcVFIzZdX.99. https://www.brainyquote.com/search_results.html?q=joubert.

[33] Most recently, Russ Lockhart and Paco Mitchell speak of this phenomenon beautifully in throughout their book *Dreams, Bones, and the Future,* (Everett, WA and Santa Fe, NM: Owl and Heron Press, 2015). See also, Sonu Shamdasani and James Hillman who speak of this notion throughout their book *Lament of the Dead,* (New York, WW. Norton & Company, 2013). These books offer valuable perspective if you are open to a more generative sense of death and grief than you may now have.

[34] James Hillman, *Re-Visioning Psychology.* The entirety of the book expresses a major paradigmatic shift in the field of psychology.

[35] James Hillman, *The Dream and the Underworld,* 39 (New York: Harper & Row, 1979), 39.

[36] *Ibid.*

[37] *Ibid.*

[38] Joseph Krutch, Porter, Brower, *Baja California and the Geography of Hope,* (San Francisco: Sierra Club/Ballantine Books, 1969).

[39] Sarah Johnston, *Hekate Soteira, op.cit.,* Fragments 35, 49, 50; 50.

[40] *Ibid.,* Fragment 35, 49.

[41] *Ibid.,* Fragment 34, 50.

[42] I*bid.,* 51

[43] *Ibid.,* Fragment 23, 55.

[44] Russell Lockhart, personal correspondence, January 1992.

[45] Russell Lockhart, Paco Mitchell, *Dreams, Bones and the Future,* 12. *op.cit.* 12

[46] Sarah Johnston, *Hekate Soteira, op.cit.* 39.

[47] *Ibid.,* 38-39. Proclus, a 5th-century Platonist.

[48] *Ibid.,* 39.

[49] *Ibid.,* 39-40.

[50] *Ibid.,* 40.

[51] *Ibid.,* 40.

[52] *Ibid.,* 42, note 36.

[53] *Ibid.,* 41.

[54] Sarah Johnston, *Hekate Soteira, op.cit.,* 39.

[55] *Ibid.,* 40-41. Author's inference made from Johnston's research.

[56] Lacy and Einarson trans of this passage in Sarah Johnston, *Hekate Soteira,* 43.

[57] *Ibid.,* 46.

[58] Proclus quoted in Sarah Johnston, *Hekate Soteira,* 45.

[59] *Ibid.,* 47.

[60] Amercan Heritage Dictionary, *op. cit.*

[61] Porphyry, ap. Eus. PE III. 11, 113 c-d in Johnston, *Hekate Soteria,* n 22.

[62] William Shakespeare, "Macbeth," Act I, Scene 3.

[63] Carl Kerenyi, *Gods of the Greeks,* (New York: Thames & Hudson, 1980), 31.

[64] Adam McLean, *The Triple Goddess, (*Hermetic Research Series, 1983, 15. Waiting for response from author

[65] Diane di Prima, *Dinners and Nightmares,* (New York, Corinth Books, 1974), 125-126.

[66] Lewis Hyde, *The Gift: Imagination and the Erotic Life of Property,* (New York, Vintage Books, 1983.)

[67] Sarah Johnston, *Hekate Soteira, op. cit.,* 31.

[68] The *daemones* are described by Empedocles as being driven up and down between Earth and Sun in recompense for their actions. Plutarch stresses the mediating nature of the daemones as an interpretive and ministering race; they convey the prayers and petitions of men to the gods, and oracles and gifts of the gods to men.

[69] Xenocrates in Sarah Johnston, *Hekate Soteria*, op.cit., 32

[70] Ibid., 33

[71] Adam McLean, The Triple Goddess, op.cit., 117.

[72] James Hillman, *The Thought of the Heart and the Soul of the World*, (Thompson Connecticut, Spring Publications, 1981), 29.

[73] John Maxwell Evans, *Lyra Graeca*, Fragment 24, (New York, G. P. Putnam and Sons, 1922.); *Sappho The poems of Sappho*, trans. John Powell,

[74] Endnote No 38 in James Hillman, *The Thought of the Heart and the Soul of the World*, op.cit., 82.

[75] James Hillman, *The Thought of the Heart and the Soul of the World*, Ibid., 29.

[76] Adam McLean, *The Triple Goddess*, op.cit., 68. Emily Vermeule, *Aspects of Death in Early Greek Art and Poetry*, (Berkeley, University of California Press, 1979), 24;
James Hillman, *The Thought of the Heart and the Soul of the World*, op. cit., 29.

[78] Erwin Rohde, *Psyche*, (New York: Harper & Row), 1966, 6.

[79] Charles Olsen, *Sulphur Anthology*, vol. 16, 96.

[80] Jane Harrison, *Prolegomena to the Study of Greek Religion*, (Princeton New Jersey, Princeton University Press, 1991), chapter 5

[81] Robert Graves, *The Greek Myths*, (Baltimore, Penguin Books, 1955), 17, 244.

[82] Porphyry in Sarah Johnston, *Hekate Soteira*, op.cit., 38.

[83] Alfred Lord Tennyson, *Maud and Other Poems*, (Boston, Tichnor & Fields, 1855), 7.

[84] The relationship with this dance and the Otherworld is inferred based on stated ties between the ancient dances and, for example, the Farondole, a French form developed in later times.

[85] Plutarch in Sarah Johnston, *Hekate Soteira*, op.cit., 38.

[86] Ibid.

[87] Sarah Johnston, *Hekate Soteira*, Ibid., 3738.

[88] Ibid.

[89] Ibid.

[90] Ibid.

[91] Sarah Johnston, *Hekate Soteira*, 38.

[92] Ibid.

[93] Ibid.

[94] Ibid.

[95] Ibid., 147.

[96] Nathan SchwartzSalant, *The Borderline Personality: Vision and Healing*, (Asheville N.C., Chiron Publications, 1989), 194.

[97] Randolph Charlton, "Lines and Shadows: Fictions from the Borderline," *The Borderline Personality in Analysis*, (Asheville N.C., Chiron Publications, 1988), 4174.

[98] Nathan SchwartzSalant, *The Borderline Personality: Vision and Healing*, 6. op. cit., 192.

[99] Ibid., 192.

[100] Ibid., 192.

[101] Sarah Johnston, *Hekate Soteira*, op.cit., 60.

[102] Andrew Samuels, *Bani Shorter, Fred Plaut, A Critical Dictionary of Jungian Analysis*, (New York, Routledge & Keegan, 1986).
Also, see C.G. Jung, *Collected Works*, Vol. 11 (Princeton New Jersey, Princeton University Press, 2014), para. 6.

[103] Nathan SchwartzSalant, *The Borderline Personality: Vision and Healing*, Chiron Publications, 1989, op. cit. 6.
104 Charles Boer, *The Homeric Hymns*, (Dunquin, Ireland, Dunquin Series, 1998), 129.

[105] Nathan SchwartzSalant, *The Borderline Personality: Vision and Healing*, op.cit. 221.

[106] Sarah Johnston, *Hekate Soteira*, op. cit. 9293

[107] Ibid., 78.

[108] Ibid., 7879.

[109] Ibid., 87.

[110] The entire body of Jung's and Lockhart's writings impart this idea. For the most recent context of this inner experience, see Lockhart's Psyche Speaks, his internet blog, "RAL's Notebook," and Dreams, Bones and the Future, coauthored with Paco Mitchell.

[111] Sarah Johnston, *Hekate Soteira*, op.cit. 82.

[112] Ibid., n16, Fragment 224, 82.

[113] Eusebius in Sarah Johnston, *Hekate Soteira*, Fragment 224, 130, op.cit.

[114] Ibid., Fragment 163, 82.

[115] Ibid., Fragment 172, 83.

[116] Russ Lockhart, in conversation, 2016.

[117] Sarah Johnston, 130-131.

[118] Ibid.,131, n202d.

[119] Psellus in Sarah Johnston, *Hekate Soteira*, op. cit.90.

[120] Damacious in Sarah Johnston, *Hekate Soteira*, 90.

[121] Sarah Johnston, *Hekate Soteira*, op. cit. n49, 108-110.

[122] Ibid, 106-110.

[123] Film by Peter Brooks (based on the book by G.I. Gurdjieff), "Meetings with Remarkable Men," Remar Studios, 1979

[124] Sarah Johnston, *Hekate Soteira*, op.cit. n17, 95.

[125] Ibid., 132.

[126] Ibid., Fragment 146, 111.

[127] Ibid., Fragment 147, 111.

[128] Ibid., Fragment 148, 111.

[129] James Hillman, *The Dream and the Underworld*, op.cit., 42. Ibid., 69.

[130] Erwin Rohde, *Psyche*, op. cit., 590.

[131] John Hastings, John Alexander Selbie, Louis Herbert Gray, Eds. *Encyclopedia of Religion: Fiction to Hyksos*, (Edinburgh, T&T Clark, 1914), 567.

[132] Callimachus, Diana, Callimachus: *Hymns and Epigrams, Lycophron and Aratus* (Harvard University, Loeb Classical Library No. 129, 1921).

[133] Joan Chamberlain. Engelsman, *The Feminine Dimension of the Divine*, (Asheville NC, Chiron, 1987), 5458. Also see Jane Harrison *Prolegomena to the Study of Greek Religion*. (Princeton: Princeton University Press, 1991)

[134] Helen Luke, *Woman Earth and Spirit,* (New York, Crossroad Publishing Co., 1984), 55.

[135] *American Heritage Dictionary*, (Boston:, Houghton Mifflin) 3rd edition, 2191.

[136] The Persian poet Rumi speaks of the Friend throughout his poetry. See, for one, *The Complete Rumi*. Trans. Coleman Barks. (San Francisco: HarperOne, 2004). Also, Aftab Omer, Founder and President of Meridian University, Petaluma, CA, who developed Transformative Learning Praxis, uses this term as a construct for his imaginal method

[137] Bill Holm, *The Music of Failure*, (Minneapolis MN, University of Minnesota Press, 1985). See first the essay "The Music of Failure."

[138] Russell Lockhart, Psyche Speaks: *A Jungian Approach to Self and World*, op. cit., 32.

[139] This paragraph on commitment is attributed to Johann Wolfgang von Goethe. However, if you consult the Goethe Society of North America online you will find that Goethe only said it "in a way." goethesociety.org/pages/quotes.com.html. W.H. Murray is the author.

[140] Robert Bly, *Leaping Poetry*, (Pittsburgh, University of Pittsburgh Press, 1975), 1.

[141] T. S. Eliot, *Collected Poems, 1909-1962*. (New York, Harcourt, Brace, Jovanovich,1963),180.

[142] Charles Boer, *The Homeric Hymns*. op. cit., 91.

[143] Leonard Cohen, "The Future" (Studio album), Columbia Records, 1992.

[144] Callimachus in Sarah Johnston, *Hekate Soteira*, op.cit. Fragment 461.

[145] Walter Burkhert, *Homo Necans*, (Berkeley, University of California Press, 1986) 64.

[146] Robert Bly, "Gravity" (poem). On Earth (magazine), http://archive.onearth.org/print/1981

[147] Robert Bly, "On Assateague Island". Reprinted from *Holes the Crickets Have Eaten in Blankets*, (Rochester, NY: Boa Editions, Ltd. 1997). Copyright 1997 Robert Bly. Used with his permission.

[148] Eduardo Galeano, lecture, Herbst Theater, San Francisco, 1993.

[149] 152 William Blake, "Auguries of Innocence." (New York, Viking Press,1950).

[150] Joan Chodorow, *To Move and Be Moved Quadrant*, 1984, 39.

[151] Verena Kast, *Joy, nspiration, Hope*: (College Station, Texas, Texas A & M University Press, 1991), 139.

[152] Ibid., 116.

[153]Ibid.

[154] Rainer Maria Rilke, *Duino Elegies*, (New York, W. W. Norton & Co., 1939), 10.

[155] Charles Olson in conversation with Robert Duncan and Allen Ginsberg, *Sulfur Anthology*, v. 33, 1993.

[156] Ibid.

[157] James Hillman, *The Thought of the Heart and the Soul of the World*, 3, op. cit., 9.

[158] Ibid. 9

[159] Natalie Goldberg, *Writing Down the Bones*, (Boulder Colo: Shambhala Publications, 1986), 107.

[160] *American Heritage Dictionary*, (NewYork,Houghton Mifflin Company, 2006),1234, 1721

[161] Quote by Marie Louise von Franz in Peter Birkhauser, *The Light in the Darkness*, (Leipzig Germany Deutsche NationalBibliotek, 1991), 4243.

[162] James Hillman, *Dream Animals*, (San Francisco, Chronicle Books, 1997).

[163] James Hillman *The Thought of the Heart and the Soul of the World*, op. cit. 10.

[164] Pablo Neruda, *The Bestiary/Bestiario*, (New York: Harcourt, Brace & World, 1965)

[165] Barbara Hannah, *The Cat, dog, and Horse Lectures*, Ed. Dean L. Frantz (Ashville, NC: Chiron Books, 1992) 70; Patricia DaleGreen, op. cit. 39, 41

[166] Alfred Huang, *The I Ching*. (Rochester Vt., Inner Traditions, 1998).

[167] Robert Graves, *The Greek Myths*, op.cit. 130

[168] Sarah Johnston, *Hekate Soteira*, op.cit. 134

[169] Emily Vermeule, *Aspects of Death in Earl,Greek Art and Poetry*, (Berkeley, University of California Press, 1979), ß3941.

[170] Ibid., 40

[171] Ibid., 40.

[172] Ibid. 41.

[173] Russell Lockhart, "Ral's Notebook," blog post, 2016. Online acccess: http://ralockhart.com/WP/

[174] *American Heritage Dictionary,* op. cit. 220.

[175] Henry David Thoreau. *Walden: Or Life in the Woods and On the Duty of Civil Disobdience*. (Mineola, NY: Dover Publications, 1995)

[176] Sarah Johnston, op. cit.

[177] Eleanor Woloy, *Symbol of the Dog in the Human Psyche* (Asheville NC, Chiron publications, 1990).

[178] C. G. Jung, 1963. par. 174, n. 280.

[179] Eleanor Woloy, op.cit., 13.

[180] C. G. Jung, 1956, 261.

[181] Barbara Hannah, op. cit.

[182] Eleanor Woloy, op. cit. 26.

[183] Ibid., 42.

[184] Diane Di Prima, *Loba, Part 1*, excerpts (New York,Penguin/Random House, December 1973).

[185] Patricia DaleGreen, *The Archetypal Cat*, op. cit., 44.

[186] Ibid.

[187] Ibid., 6869.

[188] Ibid., 45.

[189] Ibid., 45.

[190] Ibid., 46.

[191] MarieLouise von Franz, 1978.

[192] Patricia DaleGreen, op. cit., 156.

[193] Emily Dickinson, *Selected Poems and Letters of Emily Dickinson*, Ed. Robert N. Linscott (New York: Anchor Books/Doubleday, 1959), 79.

[194] Juan Edward Cirlot, *The Dictionary of Symbols*, Philosophical Library, 1062, 71.

[195] Sarah Johnston, *Hekate Sotiera*, op. cit., III.

[196] Meister Eckhart in Peter Birkhauser, *Light from the Darkness* (self published), 1980.

[197] Patricia Berry, *Echo's Subtle Body*, (Thompson CT Spring Publications, 1982), 156157.

[198] Ibid., 156

[199] Ibid., 156

[200] Ibid., 157

[201] Carl Kerenyi, *Essays on a Science of Mythology*. "The Myth of the Kore," (Princeton: University of Princeton Press, 1955), 54.

[202] *Field Guide to Birds of North America*. New York, Western Publishing Co., 1966).

[203] Carl Kerenyi, op. cit., 54.

[204] *American Heritage Dictionary*, op. cit. 680, 1543.

[205] T. S. Eliot, *Four Quartets*, (New York, Harcourt Brace, 1943), 29.

[206] Ibid., 32.

[208] Betty Smith, in conversation in Malibu, California February 1993.

[209] Nathan Schwartz – Salant Murray Stein and Nathan Schwartz Salant, *The Borderline Personality in Analysis*, (Asheville N.C., Chiron Clinical Series, 1988).

[210] *American Heritage Dictionary* HD, Ibid. op. cit., 280.)

[211] Verena Kast, *Joy, Inspiration Hope*, (College Station, Texas A&M University, 2003) 116.

[212] Ibid.

[213] Sarah Johnston, Fragment 146, op. cit., 111.

[214] There are great parenting resources now for every developmental age. Check *Positive Parenting; for teens*, visit the website of Dr. Mark Schillinger: challengingteenagesons.com, and research the *Young Men's Ultimate Weekend*; there are many options for supporting boys' wellbeing.

[215] Rainer Maria Rilke in Robert Bly, *The Winged Energy of Delight*, Selected translations (New York: Harper Perennial, 2004), 5. Ibid., 7.

[216] Frances Mayes, in Martha Vanceburg, *A New Life: Daily Readings for a Happy, Healthy Pregnancy* (New York: Bantam, 1990).

[217] Alfred Huang, *I Ching: The Book of Changes*, Hexagram/Gua #65. (Rochester Vt., Inner Traditions 1988)

[218] Russell Lockhart, Psyche Speaks: *A Jungian Approach to Self and World*, op. cit., 2015, 23.

[219] Manuel de Falla, in *Federico Garcia Lorca*, "Poem of the Deep Song," (San Francisco, City Lights,1954), 43.

[220] Ibid.

[221] Ibid., 46.

[222] Federico Garcia Lorca, *Theory and Play of the Duende* (lecture, Buenos Aires, 1933), 5051.

[223] Ibid., T.S. Eliot, *The Collected Poems 1909-1962*. "The Dry Salvages."(New York: Harcourt, Brace & Co.) 191.

[224] Rainer Maria Rilke: *Letters to a Young Poet*. (New York: W.W, Norton & Company, 1954)

[225] Natalie Goldberg, *Wild Mind: Living the Writer's Life*, (New York, Bantam Books, 1990.

[226] Olaf Hauge, "Don't Tell me the Entire Truth," in Robert Bly, *The Winged Energy of Delight*, Selected Translations, (New York, Harper Perennial Books, 2004).

[227] Charlene Spretnak: "[The] goal of feminist spirituality has never been the substitution of Yahwehinaskirt. Rather, it seeks, in all its diversity, to revitalize rational, body honoring, cosmologically grounded spiritual possibilities for women [and men]. *The Politics of Women's Spirituality*. (New York: Anchor Publishers, (1982), 128.

[228] Muriel Rukeyser says that if one woman told the truth about her life, the world would split open. Muriel Rukeyser, "Kathe Kollwitz" from *The Collected Poems of Muriel Rukeyser*, (Pittsburgh, University of Pittsburgh press, 2006), reprinted by permission of International Creative Management.

[229] Diane Di Prima, San Francisco Poet Laureate.

[230] Virgil, *Aeneid, VI*, Trans. by H.R. Fairclough. (Cambridge, MA: Loeb Classical Library, Harvard University Press, 1918) 12629. 12629, Trans. by H.R. Fairclough.

[231] T. S. Eliot, *Four Quartets*, 1943 (1971), 59.

[232] Ibid.

Image credits

Complete details for the image credits can be obtained at [LINK]

Book Cover Image: Jim Shubin altered digital image. Hekate, Digital image. World History Archive / Alamy Stock Photo. http://www.alamy.com/stock-photo-hecate.

Fig. 1. Shira Marin. Hekate Virginae. 2017.

Fig. 2. Ulricus Molitoris. Witches Add Ingredients to a Cauldron. 1489, Wikimedia Commons.

Fig. 3. Shira Marin. Active Imagination I. 1984.

Fig. 4. John Gregory (1879-1958). MacBeth with the Three Witches. Permission: Folger Shakespeare Library.

Fig. 5. Stéphane Mallarmé. Three-formed Hecate. 1880, Wikimedia Commons

Fig. 6. John William Godward, Dolce Far Niente. 1904, Wikimedia Commons

Fig. 7. Odilon Redon, Eye-Balloon. 1898, Wikimedia Commons.

Fig. 8. Shira Marin. The Eyes Have It. 1993, Tempera on paper.

Fig. 9. Shira Marin. Animal Fingers: A Vision. 1988, Mixed media on paper.

Fig. 10. Paul Klee. Above the Mountain Peaks. 1917, Haags Gemeentemuseum, The Hague, Netherlands. Permission: Maurice Tuchman. The Spiritual in Art, Plate 8.

Fig. 12. Hilma af Klint. Portfolio #5. 1920, Maurice Tuchman. The Spiritual in Art.

Fig. 13. ReptOn1x. Key from the later medieval period (1066-1500), Photo. Wikimedia Commons.

Fig. 14. Stéphane Mallarmé. Three-formed Hecate. Modified by Shira Marin, 2017. Wikimedia Commons

Fig. 15. Anonymous. Statue of Hecate (3rd century A.D.) 123RF Stock Photo.

Fig. 16. Unknown. Marble statuette of triple-bodied Hekate and the three Graces, Metropolitan Museum of Art, New York. The Bothmer Purchase Fund, 1987.

Fig. 17. Claude Bragdon. A Primer of Higher Space. 1913. Maurice Tuchman. The Spiritual in Art. Los Angeles County Museum of Art.

Fig. 18. William-Adolphe Bouguereau. The Remorse of Orestes. Wikimedia Commons.

Fig. 19. Shira Marin. Hekate Triangulata. 1990, Graphite on paper.

Fig. 20. Holly Reppert. Untitled. 1987. Watercolor and pen on paper.

Fig. 21. Unknown. Goddess Kourotrophos Seated. From: Boston Museum of Fine Art.

Fig. 22. Unknown, c620 B.C. The Gorgon Medusa Holding Pegasus. Terracotta metope, Syracuse, c620 B.C. Archiv Gerstenberg - ullstein bild / Granger, NYC.

Fig. 23. Unknown. Women's Circle Dance, Bronze Age rock art. Zerovschan, Tajikistan, Central Asia. From: http://www.sourcememory.net/veleda/?p=385

Fig. 24. Unknown, Tombstone of the Hecate Mysteries, Phrygia. From: Joscelyn Godwin. Mystery Religions in the Ancient World. New York: HarperCollins, 1982.

Fig. 25. Igor Korionov. Seven phases of the moon changes. 123RF Stock Photo

Fig. 26. Paul Serusier, The Origins. 1910, Maurice Tuchman. The Spiritual in Art.

Fig. 27. Quinn Dombrowski. Janus. Flickr Stock Photo

Fig. 28. Alexander Dmitrievich Litovchenko. Charon carries souls across the river Styx. 1861, Wikimedia Commons.

Fig. 29. Triple Hecate. Miniature bronze altar. From: Joscelyn Godwin. Mystery Religions in the Ancient World. New York: HarperCollins, 1982.

Fig. 30. Shira Marin. After Magic Words. 2016. Photo of assemblage.

Fig. 31. Shira Marin. Hekate's Iynx: from a dream. 1986.

Fig. 32. Shira Marin. At your Beck and Call: Active Imagination. 1987.

Fig. 33. Paul Ranson. The Sorceresses. 1891. Adapted by Shira Marin. From: Maurice Tuchman. The Spiritual in Art: Abstract Painting 1890-1985. Los Angeles: Los Angeles County Museum of Art, 1989. Plate 14.

Fig. 34. Shira Marin. Getting Ready for Hekate.

Fig. 35. Sailko. Hekataion from the Temple of Atena Polias. Wikimedia Commons

Fig. 36. Daderot. The Bath. Jean-Leon Gerome, 1870. Wikimedia Commons.

Fig. 37. Peter Birkhauser. Isis. 1976, Litho. Plate 37. Permission: Springer Basel AG; permission conveyed through Copyright Clearance Center, Inc.

Fig. 38. Shira Marin. Hekate Supper.

Fig. 39. Anonymous. Untitled. 1984.

Fig. 40. Piet Mondrian. Spring. 1906, From: Maurice Tuchman. The Spiritual in Art.

Fig. 61. Hans Beham. Hercules Capturing Cerberus, 1545, Wikimedia Commons.

Fig. 62. Bibi Saint-Pol, 2007. Hekate Thanatoio-Eos, signed Douris (painter) and Kalliades (potter), 490-80 BC. Musée du Louvre, Paris, France. Wikimedia Commons

Fig. 63. Shira Marin. Ker Thanatoio. 1986.

Fig. 64. William Blake, First Version of Cerberus,1827, Wikimedia Commons.

Fig. 65. Unknown. Ginger. 1991. Altered photograph of author's Chow Chow.

Fig. 66. Marie-Lan Nguyen, 2011.'Cave canem' (beware of the dog) mosaic. Pompeii, Casa di Orfeo, VI.14.20. Wikimedia Commons.

Fig. 67. Christel Neldner, Howling Wolf. 1979. Altered by Shira Marin. Artist permission. christel@pyramid.net

Fig. 68. Late Period-Ptolemaic Period Egypt (Brooklyn Mus.) Wikimedia Commons.

Fig. 69. Ancient papyrus, Cat Goddess Killing the Evil Snake God Apep, 1300 BCE. Available from:
http://www.landofpyramids.org/images/bastet-apep.jpg

Fig. 70. Unknown. Canopic Jar with Cat. Online access: July 30, 2017

Fig. 71. Einsamer Schütze. The Gayer-Anderson Cat. Photo 2011. British Museum, Wikimedia Commons.

Fig. 72. Mitsuaki Iwago. African Lion (Pantera Leo) with cub. Permission: National Geographic. May, 1986.

Fig. 73. Malgorzata Kistryn. Sculpture of emblem of India. Malabar Hill, Mumbai, India. 123RF Stock Photo.

Fig. 74. Holly Reppert, Untitled. 1986. Artist permission.

Fig. 75. Hilma af Klint, Svanen, 1914. Wikimedia Commons.

Fig. 76. Shira Marin, Hekate Holy Wingedness I. 2017.

Fig. 77. Franco Atirador, Raven Croak. 2007. Wikimedia Commons.

Fig. 78. Ogata Korin, Crows and Moon. 1658-1716. Woodblock print. From the Robert Muller Estate. Internet, Accessed April, 2017.

Fig. 79. Unknown, Girl with the Horse and the Rose.

Fig. 80. Shira Marin. Medusa with Horse, Bird, and Egg. 1986.

Fig. 81. Annie Danberg, (graphic design) and Shira Marin, image design. Mute Swan Press logo. Digital image, 2017.

Fig. 82. Jeremy Johnson. Mute Swan. 2016. Permission of the owner.

Fig. 83. Edvard Munch, The Voice, Summer Night. 1863-1944.Munch Museum, Oslo, Norway. Wikimedia Commons.

Fig. 84. Theodotus and Pytheos. Tetradrachm if Klazomenai with Swan. c. 375-370 B.C. Greek coin; silver. http://www.mfa.org. Accession number: 08.329; April, 2017.

Fig. 85. Shira Marin. Hekate Angelos, (Detail) II. 2016.

Fig. 86. Bibi Saint-Pol. Zeus Typhon. Chalkidian pottery. Wikimedia Commons

Fig. 87. Sulamith Wulfing. Dark Wings, 1951, Litho. Accessed online: April, 2017.

Fig. 88. Shira Marin. Tangerine Mother. 2008. Altered image with watercolor, ink, and graphite on paper; 8 x 12 inches.

Fig. 89. Betty Decter. Dreams and Other-Transformations. 1984. By permission of Karalee Fenske, Representative of the Est. of Betty Decter, www.karaleepf@aol.com

Fig. 90. Ernst Nay. Daughter of Hekate, © 1945 Elisabeth Nay-Scheibler, Köln / Artists Rights Society (ARS), New York.

Fig. 91. Shira Marin. Veiled Hekate. 1986, Polaroid photo.

Fig. 92. Frantisek Kupka. Der Traum (The Dream). 1909, Maurice Tuchman. The Spiritual in Art. Los Angeles County Museum of Art, 1989. Plate 9.

Fig. 94. The author with her father. 1953. Black and white photograph.

Fig. 95. Shira Marin. Mother and Child: Reborn. 1989. Handmade paper, acrylic paint.

The Author

Shira Marin, PhD, a Licensed Marriage and Family Therapist for more than 35 years, is also an educator, speaker, writer, and artist intimately engaged with the psychoactive nature of life. In her private practice, Dr. Marin serves individuals, couples, families, and groups through the lens of Jungian Psychology and consults to clinicians and interns. Her primary interests focus on the individual and society, consultancy to groups and communities, and developing collective, collaborative peace-making processes through the engagement of non-violent communication, imagination, and feminine values.

Dr. Marin is the immediate past president of the Northern California Group Psychotherapy Society and served as adjunct faculty of John F. Kennedy University and the Community Institute for Psychotherapy. She lives in Marin County with her family and their standard poodle, Bella Rosa, who assists Dr. Marin in the consulting room.

CPSIA information can be obtained
at www.ICGtesting.com
Printed in the USA
LVHW080255221119
638114LV00006B/59/P

9 780998 661551